JAMESTOWN EDUCATION

Reading Fluency

Reader's Record

Level
G

Camille L. Z. Blachowicz, Ph.D.

JAMESTOWN ⛵ EDUCATION

Reading Fluency

Reader's Record

Level
G

Camille L. Z. Blachowicz, Ph.D.

Mc Graw Hill **Glencoe**

New York, New York   Columbus, Ohio   Chicago, Illinois   Peoria, Illinois   Woodland Hills, California

JAMESTOWN EDUCATION

Glencoe

The McGraw·Hill Companies

Send all inquiries to:
Glencoe/McGraw-Hill
8787 Orion Place
Columbus, OH 43240-4027

ISBN 0-07-845704-1
Printed in the United States of America.
  6 7 8 9 10   021   09 08

Contents

The passages in this book are taken from the following sources.

How to Use These Books

The Reading Fluency *Reader* contains 72 reading passages. The accompanying *Reader's Record* contains two copies of each of these passages and includes a place for marking *miscues*. You and your partner will take turns using the *Reader*. Each of you will need your own *Reader's Record*. You will also need a stopwatch or a timer.

What Are Miscues?

Miscues are errors or slips that all readers make. These include the following:
- a mispronounced word
- a word substituted for the correct word
- an inserted word
- a skipped word

Repeating a word or correcting oneself immediately is not counted as a miscue.

What Procedure Do I Follow?

1. Work with a partner. One partner is the reader; the other partner is the recorder.

2. Suppose that you are the first to read aloud. Read a selection from the *Reader* as your partner marks any miscues you make on the corresponding page in your *Reader's Record*. The recorder's job is to listen carefully and make a tick mark above each place in the text where a miscue occurs, and to make a slash mark indicating where you stop reading after "Time!" is called.

3. The recorder says when to start and calls "Time!" after a minute.

4. After the reading, the recorder:
- counts the number of words read, using the number guides at the right-hand side of the passage, and records the Total Words Read
- writes the total number of miscues for each line in the far right-hand column labeled Miscues. Totals and records the miscues on the Total Errors line
- subtracts Total Errors from Total Words Read to find the Correct Words Per Minute (WPM) and records that score on the Correct WPM line

5. You review the *Reader's Record*, noting your miscues. Discuss with your partner the characteristics of good reading you have displayed. Then rate your own performance and mark the scale at the bottom of the page.

6. Change roles with your partner and repeat the procedure.

7. You and your partner then begin a second round of reading the same passage. When it is your turn to read, try to improve in pace, expression, and accuracy over the first reading.

8. After completing two readings, record your Correct WPM scores in the back of your *Reader's Record*. Follow the directions on the graph.

		First Reading

1 Nonfiction

from *Undying Glory*
by Clinton Cox

	Words Read	Miscues

⊶⊷

	Words Read	Miscues
Shaw led the way, accompanied by engineers who knew	9	_____
the terrain. The march was like a nightmare for the tired and	21	_____
hungry soldiers.	23	_____
Lewis Douglass later wrote his father: "That night we took,	33	_____
according to one of our officers, one of the hardest marches on	45	_____
record, through woods and marsh."	50	_____
A strong wind constantly drove the rain against their faces,	60	_____
and the path grew steadily narrower. At first two men could walk	72	_____
[together], then the path was barely wide enough for one.	82	_____
The only light was from lightning flashes, and each man had	93	_____
to hold onto the man in front of him as they inched their way	107	_____
across swaying planks spanning long stretches of deep water. The	117	_____
rickety little bridges had no handrails and soon became slippery	127	_____
with mud.	129	_____
Often the men fell in, and had to struggle furiously to raise	141	_____
themselves back onto the planks. Soon their clothes and bodies	151	_____
were soaked with stagnant swamp water.	157	_____
All night thunder sounded like a mournful drum, and the quick	168	_____
flashes of lightning left them groping in darkness that seemed	178	_____
even blacker than before.	182	_____
The ground was soaked and the soles of their boots were soon	194	_____
covered with big lumps of clay. When they left a swamp and	206	_____
entered woods, the branches slapped at their hands and faces.	216	_____

Needs Work   1   2   3   4   5   Excellent
Paid attention to punctuation

Needs Work   1   2   3   4   5   Excellent
Sounded good

Total Words Read _____

Total Errors − _____

Correct WPM _____

1

from *Undying Glory*
by Clinton Cox

	Words Read	Miscues

Shaw led the way, accompanied by engineers who knew   9   _____
the terrain. The march was like a nightmare for the tired and   21   _____
hungry soldiers.   23   _____

Lewis Douglass later wrote his father: "That night we took,   33   _____
according to one of our officers, one of the hardest marches on   45   _____
record, through woods and marsh."   50   _____

A strong wind constantly drove the rain against their faces,   60   _____
and the path grew steadily narrower. At first two men could walk   72   _____
[together], then the path was barely wide enough for one.   82   _____

The only light was from lightning flashes, and each man had   93   _____
to hold onto the man in front of him as they inched their way   107   _____
across swaying planks spanning long stretches of deep water. The   117   _____
rickety little bridges had no handrails and soon became slippery   127   _____
with mud.   129   _____

Often the men fell in, and had to struggle furiously to raise   141   _____
themselves back onto the planks. Soon their clothes and bodies   151   _____
were soaked with stagnant swamp water.   157   _____

All night thunder sounded like a mournful drum, and the quick   168   _____
flashes of lightning left them groping in darkness that seemed   178   _____
even blacker than before.   182   _____

The ground was soaked and the soles of their boots were soon   194   _____
covered with big lumps of clay. When they left a swamp and   206   _____
entered woods, the branches slapped at their hands and faces.   216   _____

Needs Work 1 2 3 4 5 **Excellent**
Paid attention to punctuation

Needs Work 1 2 3 4 5 **Excellent**
Sounded good

Total Words Read _____

Total Errors − _____

Correct WPM _____

2 from **"Waiting"**
by Budge Wilson

Fiction

	Words Read	Miscues

The play we put on in 1942 was about a rich nobleman called | 13 | _____
Alphonse who falls in love with an exquisitely beautiful but | 23 | _____
humble country girl called Genevieve. I played the part of | 33 | _____
Genevieve, and it was the nicest part I had ever played. In the last | 47 | _____
scene, Genevieve and the nobleman become engaged, and she | 56 | _____
gets to dress up in a very gorgeous gown for a big court ball. I | 71 | _____
had a real dress for this scene, instead of the usual pieced- | 83 | _____
together scraps of material dug out of old trunks from our attics. | 94 | _____
My mother let me use one of her long dance dresses from when | 107 | _____
she was young. It was covered with sequins and even had some | 119 | _____
sort of fluffy feather stuff around the hem; and it was pale | 131 | _____
sapphire blue and very romantic looking. I had trouble getting | 141 | _____
into it because I was almost thirteen now and sort of big through | 154 | _____
the middle. But my mother put in a new zipper instead of the | 167 | _____
buttons, and I was able to wear it after all. I had to move a little | 183 | _____
carefully and not take very deep breaths, but I was as tall as | 196 | _____
Mama now, and I felt like a real woman, a true beauty. | 208 | _____

Needs Work   1   2   3   4   5   Excellent
Paid attention to punctuation

Needs Work   1   2   3   4   5   Excellent
Sounded good

Total Words Read _____

Total Errors − _____

Correct WPM _____

3

from "Waiting"

by Budge Wilson

	Words Read	Miscues
The play we put on in 1942 was about a rich nobleman called	13	_____
Alphonse who falls in love with an exquisitely beautiful but	23	_____
humble country girl called Genevieve. I played the part of	33	_____
Genevieve, and it was the nicest part I had ever played. In the last	47	_____
scene, Genevieve and the nobleman become engaged, and she	56	_____
gets to dress up in a very gorgeous gown for a big court ball. I	71	_____
had a real dress for this scene, instead of the usual pieced-	83	_____
together scraps of material dug out of old trunks from our attics.	94	_____
My mother let me use one of her long dance dresses from when	107	_____
she was young. It was covered with sequins and even had some	119	_____
sort of fluffy feather stuff around the hem; and it was pale	131	_____
sapphire blue and very romantic looking. I had trouble getting	141	_____
into it because I was almost thirteen now and sort of big through	154	_____
the middle. But my mother put in a new zipper instead of the	167	_____
buttons, and I was able to wear it after all. I had to move a little	183	_____
carefully and not take very deep breaths, but I was as tall as	196	_____
Mama now, and I felt like a real woman, a true beauty.	208	_____

Needs Work   1   2   3   4   5   Excellent
Paid attention to punctuation

Needs Work   1   2   3   4   5   Excellent
Sounded good

Total Words Read _____

Total Errors − _____

Correct WPM _____

3 Nonfiction

from *Anne Frank: The Diary of a Young Girl*

by Anne Frank

I have one outstanding trait in my character, which must strike	11	_____
anyone who knows me for any length of time, and that is my	24	_____
knowledge of myself. I can watch myself and my actions, just like	36	_____
an outsider. The Anne of every day I can face entirely without	48	_____
prejudice, without making excuses for her, and watch what's good	58	_____
and what's bad about her. This "self-consciousness" haunts me,	67	_____
and every time I open my mouth I know as soon as I've spoken	81	_____
whether "that ought to have been different" or "that was right as	93	_____
it was." There are so many things about myself that I condemn; I	106	_____
couldn't begin to name them all. I understand more and more	117	_____
how true Daddy's words were when he said: "All children must	128	_____
look after their own upbringing." Parents can only give good	138	_____
advice or put them on the right paths, but the final forming of a	152	_____
person's character lies in their own hands.	159	_____
In addition to this, I have lots of courage, I always feel so	172	_____
strong and as if I can bear a great deal, I feel so free and so	188	_____
young! I was glad when I first realized it, because I don't think	201	_____
I shall easily bow down before the blows that inevitably come	212	_____
to everyone.	214	_____

Needs Work   1   2   3   4   5   Excellent
Paid attention to punctuation

Needs Work   1   2   3   4   5   Excellent
Sounded good

Total Words Read _____

Total Errors − _____

Correct WPM _____

3 Nonfiction

from *Anne Frank: The Diary of a Young Girl*
by Anne Frank

	Words Read	Miscues
I have one outstanding trait in my character, which must strike	11	_____
anyone who knows me for any length of time, and that is my	24	_____
knowledge of myself. I can watch myself and my actions, just like	36	_____
an outsider. The Anne of every day I can face entirely without	48	_____
prejudice, without making excuses for her, and watch what's good	58	_____
and what's bad about her. This "self-consciousness" haunts me,	67	_____
and every time I open my mouth I know as soon as I've spoken	81	_____
whether "that ought to have been different" or "that was right as	93	_____
it was." There are so many things about myself that I condemn; I	106	_____
couldn't begin to name them all. I understand more and more	117	_____
how true Daddy's words were when he said: "All children must	128	_____
look after their own upbringing." Parents can only give good	138	_____
advice or put them on the right paths, but the final forming of a	152	_____
person's character lies in their own hands.	159	_____
In addition to this, I have lots of courage, I always feel so	172	_____
strong and as if I can bear a great deal, I feel so free and so	188	_____
young! I was glad when I first realized it, because I don't think	201	_____
I shall easily bow down before the blows that inevitably come	212	_____
to everyone.	214	_____

Needs Work   1 2 3 4 5   Excellent
Paid attention to punctuation

Needs Work   1 2 3 4 5   Excellent
Sounded good

Total Words Read _____

Total Errors − _____

Correct WPM _____

4

Fiction

from *Hatchet*

by Gary Paulsen

	Words Read	Miscues

Brian Robeson stared out the window of the small plane at | 11 | _____
the endless green northern wilderness below. It was a small plane, | 22 | _____
a Cessna 406—a bush-plane—and the engine was so loud, so | 34 | _____
roaring and consuming and loud, that it ruined any chance | 44 | _____
for conversation. | 46 | _____

Not that he had much to say. He was thirteen and the only | 59 | _____
passenger on the plane with a pilot named—what was it? Jim or | 72 | _____
Jake or something—who was in his mid-forties and who had been | 84 | _____
silent as he worked to prepare for take-off. In fact since Brian had | 97 | _____
come to the small airport in Hampton, New York to meet the | 109 | _____
plane—driven by his mother—the pilot had spoken only five | 120 | _____
words to him. | 123 | _____

"Get in the copilot's seat." | 128 | _____

Which Brian had done. They had taken off and that was the | 140 | _____
last of the conversation. There had been the initial excitement, of | 151 | _____
course. He had never flown in a single-engine plane before and to | 163 | _____
be sitting in the copilot's seat with all the controls right there in | 176 | _____
front of him, all the instruments in his face as the plane clawed | 189 | _____
for altitude, jerking and sliding on the wind currents as the pilot | 201 | _____
took off, had been interesting and exciting. | 208 | _____

Needs Work   1   2   3   4   5   Excellent
Paid attention to punctuation

Needs Work   1   2   3   4   5   Excellent
Sounded good

Total Words Read   _____

Total Errors − _____

Correct WPM   _____

4

Fiction

from *Hatchet*

by Gary Paulsen

	Words Read	Miscues

Brian Robeson stared out the window of the small plane at
the endless green northern wilderness below. It was a small plane,
a Cessna 406—a bush-plane—and the engine was so loud, so
roaring and consuming and loud, that it ruined any chance
for conversation.

Not that he had much to say. He was thirteen and the only
passenger on the plane with a pilot named—what was it? Jim or
Jake or something—who was in his mid-forties and who had been
silent as he worked to prepare for take-off. In fact since Brian had
come to the small airport in Hampton, New York to meet the
plane—driven by his mother—the pilot had spoken only five
words to him.

"Get in the copilot's seat."

Which Brian had done. They had taken off and that was the
last of the conversation. There had been the initial excitement, of
course. He had never flown in a single-engine plane before and to
be sitting in the copilot's seat with all the controls right there in
front of him, all the instruments in his face as the plane clawed
for altitude, jerking and sliding on the wind currents as the pilot
took off, had been interesting and exciting.

Words Read
11
22
34
44
46
59
72
84
97
109
120
123
128
140
151
163
176
189
201
208

Needs Work   1   2   3   4   5   Excellent
Paid attention to punctuation

Needs Work   1   2   3   4   5   Excellent
Sounded good

Total Words Read _____

Total Errors − _____

Correct WPM _____

5

Nonfiction

from *The Lost Garden*
by Laurence Yep

First Reading

	Words Read	Miscues

A small grocery store is like a big beast that must be
continually fed and cared for. Cans, packages, and bottles have to
be put on shelves to take the place of things sold, produce like
greens and celery have to be nursed along to keep them fresh as
long as possible, and there are hundreds of other details that the
customers never notice—unless they aren't done. In a small,
family-owned store, certain chores must be done at a specific
time each day. There is no choice.

Our store had its own daily rhythms just like a farm would
have. It began before eight in the morning when my mother
would pick her way down the unlit back stairs and along the dark
alleyway to the backdoor of the store. Balancing the box with the
cash register money in the crook of her arm, she would find the
keyhole by feel and let herself in. Then, going through the
darkened store, she would put the money in the cash register
drawer. There were no neat rolls of coins. Instead, she had them
each in a small paper bag, from pennies to fifty-cent pieces, and
also dollar bills and bigger denominations in separate sacks.

Words Read
12
23
36
49
61
71
81
88
100
111
124
136
149
160
171
183
195
204

Needs Work   1   2   3   4   5   Excellent
Paid attention to punctuation

Needs Work   1   2   3   4   5   Excellent
Sounded good

Total Words Read _____

Total Errors − _____

Correct WPM _____

from *The Lost Garden*
by Laurence Yep

	Words Read	Miscues

A small grocery store is like a big beast that must be · 12 · _____

continually fed and cared for. Cans, packages, and bottles have to · 23 · _____

be put on shelves to take the place of things sold, produce like · 36 · _____

greens and celery have to be nursed along to keep them fresh as · 49 · _____

long as possible, and there are hundreds of other details that the · 61 · _____

customers never notice—unless they aren't done. In a small, · 71 · _____

family-owned store, certain chores must be done at a specific · 81 · _____

time each day. There is no choice. · 88 · _____

Our store had its own daily rhythms just like a farm would · 100 · _____

have. It began before eight in the morning when my mother · 111 · _____

would pick her way down the unlit back stairs and along the dark · 124 · _____

alleyway to the backdoor of the store. Balancing the box with the · 136 · _____

cash register money in the crook of her arm, she would find the · 149 · _____

keyhole by feel and let herself in. Then, going through the · 160 · _____

darkened store, she would put the money in the cash register · 171 · _____

drawer. There were no neat rolls of coins. Instead, she had them · 183 · _____

each in a small paper bag, from pennies to fifty-cent pieces, and · 195 · _____

also dollar bills and bigger denominations in separate sacks. · 204 · _____

Needs Work   1   2   3   4   5   Excellent
Paid attention to punctuation

Needs Work   1   2   3   4   5   Excellent
Sounded good

Total Words Read   _____

Total Errors   −   _____

Correct WPM   _____

6
Fiction

from **"Chee's Daughter"**
by Juanita Platero and Siyowin Miller

	Words Read	Miscues

Chee was near the hogan on the day his cousins rode up with | 13 | _____
the message for which he waited. He had been watching with | 24 | _____
mixed emotions while his father and his sister's husband cleared | 34 | _____
the fields beside the stream. | 39 | _____

"The boss at the camp says he needs an extra hand, but he | 52 | _____
wants to know if you'll be willing to go with the camp when they | 66 | _____
move it to the other side of town?" The tall cousin shifted his | 79 | _____
weight in the saddle. | 83 | _____

The other cousin took up the explanation. "The work near here | 94 | _____
will last only until the new cutoff beyond Red Sands is finished. | 106 | _____
After that, the work will be too far away for you to get back | 120 | _____
here often." | 122 | _____

That was what Chee had wanted—to get away from Little | 133 | _____
Canyon—yet he found himself not so interested in the job | 144 | _____
beyond town as in this new cutoff which was almost finished. He | 156 | _____
pulled a blade of grass, split it thoughtfully down the center, as he | 169 | _____
asked questions of his cousins. Finally he said: "I need to think | 181 | _____
more about this. If I decide on this job, I'll ride over." | 193 | _____

Before his cousins were out of sight down the canyon, Chee | 204 | _____
was walking toward the fields, a bold plan shaping in his mind. | 216 | _____

Needs Work 1 2 3 4 5 Excellent
Paid attention to punctuation

Needs Work 1 2 3 4 5 Excellent
Sounded good

Total Words Read _____

Total Errors − _____

Correct WPM _____

6

Fiction

from "Chee's Daughter"

by Juanita Platero and Siyowin Miller

	Words Read	Miscues

Chee was near the hogan on the day his cousins rode up with | 13

the message for which he waited. He had been watching with | 24

mixed emotions while his father and his sister's husband cleared | 34

the fields beside the stream. | 39

"The boss at the camp says he needs an extra hand, but he | 52

wants to know if you'll be willing to go with the camp when they | 66

move it to the other side of town?" The tall cousin shifted his | 79

weight in the saddle. | 83

The other cousin took up the explanation. "The work near here | 94

will last only until the new cutoff beyond Red Sands is finished. | 106

After that, the work will be too far away for you to get back | 120

here often." | 122

That was what Chee had wanted—to get away from Little | 133

Canyon—yet he found himself not so interested in the job | 144

beyond town as in this new cutoff which was almost finished. He | 156

pulled a blade of grass, split it thoughtfully down the center, as he | 169

asked questions of his cousins. Finally he said: "I need to think | 181

more about this. If I decide on this job, I'll ride over." | 193

Before his cousins were out of sight down the canyon, Chee | 204

was walking toward the fields, a bold plan shaping in his mind. | 216

Needs Work 1 2 3 4 5 Excellent
Paid attention to punctuation

Needs Work 1 2 3 4 5 Excellent
Sounded good

Total Words Read _____

Total Errors − _____

Correct WPM _____

7 Fiction

from "To Build a Fire"
by Jack London

	Words Read	Miscues
Gradually, as the flame grew stronger, he increased the size of the	12	_____
twigs with which he fed it. He squatted in the snow, pulling the	25	_____
twigs out from their entanglement in the brush and feeding	35	_____
directly to the flame. He knew there must be no failure. When it	48	_____
is seventy-five below zero, a man must not fail in his first attempt	61	_____
to build a fire—that is, if his feet are wet. If his feet are dry, and	78	_____
he fails, he can run along the trail for half a mile and restore his	93	_____
circulation. But the circulation of wet and freezing feet cannot be	104	_____
restored by running when it is seventy-five below. No matter how	115	_____
fast he runs, the wet feet will freeze the harder.	125	_____
All this the man knew. The old-timer on Sulphur Creek had	136	_____
told him about it the previous fall, and now he was appreciating	148	_____
the advice. Already all sensation had gone out of his feet. To build	161	_____
the fire he had been forced to remove his mittens, and the fingers	174	_____
had quickly gone numb. His pace of four miles an hour had kept	187	_____
his heart pumping blood to the surface of his body and to all the	201	_____
extremities. But the instant he stopped, the action of the pump	212	_____
eased down.	214	_____

Needs Work   1   2   3   4   5   Excellent
Paid attention to punctuation

Needs Work   1   2   3   4   5   Excellent
Sounded good

Total Words Read _____

Total Errors − _____

Correct WPM _____

7

Fiction

from **"To Build a Fire"**
by Jack London

	Words Read	Miscues

Gradually, as the flame grew stronger, he increased the size of the | 12 | _____
twigs with which he fed it. He squatted in the snow, pulling the | 25 | _____
twigs out from their entanglement in the brush and feeding | 35 | _____
directly to the flame. He knew there must be no failure. When it | 48 | _____
is seventy-five below zero, a man must not fail in his first attempt | 61 | _____
to build a fire—that is, if his feet are wet. If his feet are dry, and | 78 | _____
he fails, he can run along the trail for half a mile and restore his | 93 | _____
circulation. But the circulation of wet and freezing feet cannot be | 104 | _____
restored by running when it is seventy-five below. No matter how | 115 | _____
fast he runs, the wet feet will freeze the harder. | 125 | _____

All this the man knew. The old-timer on Sulphur Creek had | 136 | _____
told him about it the previous fall, and now he was appreciating | 148 | _____
the advice. Already all sensation had gone out of his feet. To build | 161 | _____
the fire he had been forced to remove his mittens, and the fingers | 174 | _____
had quickly gone numb. His pace of four miles an hour had kept | 187 | _____
his heart pumping blood to the surface of his body and to all the | 201 | _____
extremities. But the instant he stopped, the action of the pump | 212 | _____
eased down. | 214 | _____

Needs Work   1 2 3 4 5   Excellent
Paid attention to punctuation

Needs Work   1 2 3 4 5   Excellent
Sounded good

Total Words Read   _____

Total Errors − _____

Correct WPM   _____

8 Nonfiction

from "Three Days to See"
by Helen Keller

	Words Read	Miscues

Now and then I have tested my seeing friends to discover   11   _____
what they see. Recently I was visited by a very good friend who   24   _____
had just returned from a long walk in the woods, and I asked her   38   _____
what she had observed. "Nothing in particular," she replied. I   48   _____
might have been incredulous had I not been accustomed to   58   _____
such responses, for long ago I became convinced that the seeing   69   _____
see little.   71   _____

How was it possible, I asked myself, to walk for an hour through   84   _____
the woods and see nothing worthy of note? I who cannot see find   97   _____
hundreds of things to interest me through mere touch. I feel the   109   _____
delicate symmetry of a leaf. I pass my hands lovingly about the   121   _____
smooth skin of a silver birch, or the rough, shaggy bark of a pine.   135   _____
In spring I touch the branches of trees hopefully in search of a   148   _____
bud, the first sign of awakening Nature after her winter's sleep. I   160   _____
feel the delightful, velvety texture of a flower, and discover its   171   _____
remarkable convolutions; and something of the miracle of Nature   180   _____
is revealed to me. Occasionally, if I am very fortunate, I place my   193   _____
hand gently on a small tree and feel the happy quiver of a bird in   208   _____
full song.   210   _____

Needs Work   1 2 3 4 5   Excellent
Paid attention to punctuation

Needs Work   1 2 3 4 5   Excellent
Sounded good

Total Words Read _____

Total Errors − _____

Correct WPM _____

8

Nonfiction

from "Three Days to See"
by Helen Keller

	Words Read	Miscues

Now and then I have tested my seeing friends to discover   11 _____
what they see. Recently I was visited by a very good friend who   24 _____
had just returned from a long walk in the woods, and I asked her   38 _____
what she had observed. "Nothing in particular," she replied. I   48 _____
might have been incredulous had I not been accustomed to   58 _____
such responses, for long ago I became convinced that the seeing   69 _____
see little.   71 _____

How was it possible, I asked myself, to walk for an hour through   84 _____
the woods and see nothing worthy of note? I who cannot see find   97 _____
hundreds of things to interest me through mere touch. I feel the   109 _____
delicate symmetry of a leaf. I pass my hands lovingly about the   121 _____
smooth skin of a silver birch, or the rough, shaggy bark of a pine.   135 _____
In spring I touch the branches of trees hopefully in search of a   148 _____
bud, the first sign of awakening Nature after her winter's sleep. I   160 _____
feel the delightful, velvety texture of a flower, and discover its   171 _____
remarkable convolutions; and something of the miracle of Nature   180 _____
is revealed to me. Occasionally, if I am very fortunate, I place my   193 _____
hand gently on a small tree and feel the happy quiver of a bird in   208 _____
full song.   210 _____

Needs Work   1 2 3 4 5   Excellent
Paid attention to punctuation

Needs Work   1 2 3 4 5   Excellent
Sounded good

Total Words Read   _____

Total Errors − _____

Correct WPM   _____

9

Nonfiction

from *Farewell to Manzanar*

by Jeanne Wakatsuki Houston and James D. Houston

First Reading

	Words Read	Miscues

I had never been outside Los Angeles County, never traveled   10   _____

more than ten miles from the coast, had never even ridden on a   23   _____

bus. I was full of excitement, the way any kid would be, and   36   _____

wanted to look out the window. But for the first few hours the   49   _____

shades were drawn. Around me other people played cards, read   59   _____

magazines, dozed, waiting. I settled back, waiting too, and finally   69   _____

fell asleep. The bus felt very secure to me. Almost half its   81   _____

passengers were immediate relatives. Mama and my older   89   _____

brothers had succeeded in keeping most of us together, on the   100   _____

same bus, headed for the same camp. I didn't realize until much   112   _____

later what a job that was. The strategy had been, first, to have   125   _____

everyone living in the same district when the evacuation began,   135   _____

and then to get all of us included under the same family number,   148   _____

even though names had been changed by marriage. Many families   158   _____

weren't as lucky as ours and suffered months of anguish while   169   _____

trying to arrange transfers from one camp to another.   178   _____

We rode all day. By the time we reached our destination, the   190   _____

shades were up. It was late afternoon.   197   _____

Needs Work   1   2   3   4   5   Excellent
Paid attention to punctuation

Needs Work   1   2   3   4   5   Excellent
Sounded good

Total Words Read _____

Total Errors − _____

Correct WPM _____

from *Farewell to Manzanar*

by Jeanne Wakatsuki Houston and James D. Houston

	Words Read	Miscues
I had never been outside Los Angeles County, never traveled	10	_____
more than ten miles from the coast, had never even ridden on a	23	_____
bus. I was full of excitement, the way any kid would be, and	36	_____
wanted to look out the window. But for the first few hours the	49	_____
shades were drawn. Around me other people played cards, read	59	_____
magazines, dozed, waiting. I settled back, waiting too, and finally	69	_____
fell asleep. The bus felt very secure to me. Almost half its	81	_____
passengers were immediate relatives. Mama and my older	89	_____
brothers had succeeded in keeping most of us together, on the	100	_____
same bus, headed for the same camp. I didn't realize until much	112	_____
later what a job that was. The strategy had been, first, to have	125	_____
everyone living in the same district when the evacuation began,	135	_____
and then to get all of us included under the same family number,	148	_____
even though names had been changed by marriage. Many families	158	_____
weren't as lucky as ours and suffered months of anguish while	169	_____
trying to arrange transfers from one camp to another.	178	_____
We rode all day. By the time we reached our destination, the	190	_____
shades were up. It was late afternoon.	197	_____

Needs Work 1 2 3 4 5 Excellent
Paid attention to punctuation

Needs Work 1 2 3 4 5 Excellent
Sounded good

Total Words Read _____

Total Errors − _____

Correct WPM _____

10 from *Sounder*
Fiction by William H. Armstrong

	Words Read	Miscues

In his lonely journeying, the boy had learned to tell himself | 11 | _____

the stories his mother had told him at night in the cabin. He liked | 25 | _____

the way they always ended with the right thing happening. And | 36 | _____

people in stories were never feared of anything. Sometimes he | 46 | _____

tried to put together things he had read in the newspapers he | 58 | _____

found and make new stories. But the ends never came out right, | 70 | _____

and they made him more afraid. The people he tried to put in | 83 | _____

stories from the papers always seemed like strangers. Some story | 93 | _____

people he wouldn't be afraid of if he met them on the road. He | 107 | _____

thought he liked the David and Joseph stories best of all. "Why | 119 | _____

you want 'em told over'n over?" his mother had asked so many | 131 | _____

times. Now, alone on a bed of pine needles, he remembered that | 143 | _____

he could never answer his mother. He would just wait, and if his | 156 | _____

mother wasn't sad, with her lips stretched thin, she would stop | 167 | _____

humming and tell about David the boy, or King David. If she felt | 180 | _____

good and started long enough before bedtime, he would hear | 190 | _____

about Joseph the slave-boy, Joseph in prison, Joseph the dreamer, | 200 | _____

and Joseph the Big Man in Egypt. | 207 | _____

Needs Work   1 2 3 4 5   Excellent
Paid attention to punctuation

Needs Work   1 2 3 4 5   Excellent
Sounded good

Total Words Read _____

Total Errors − _____

Correct WPM _____

from *Sounder*

by William H. Armstrong

	Words Read	Miscues
In his lonely journeying, the boy had learned to tell himself	11	_____
the stories his mother had told him at night in the cabin. He liked	25	_____
the way they always ended with the right thing happening. And	36	_____
people in stories were never feared of anything. Sometimes he	46	_____
tried to put together things he had read in the newspapers he	58	_____
found and make new stories. But the ends never came out right,	70	_____
and they made him more afraid. The people he tried to put in	83	_____
stories from the papers always seemed like strangers. Some story	93	_____
people he wouldn't be afraid of if he met them on the road. He	107	_____
thought he liked the David and Joseph stories best of all. "Why	119	_____
you want 'em told over'n over?" his mother had asked so many	131	_____
times. Now, alone on a bed of pine needles, he remembered that	143	_____
he could never answer his mother. He would just wait, and if his	156	_____
mother wasn't sad, with her lips stretched thin, she would stop	167	_____
humming and tell about David the boy, or King David. If she felt	180	_____
good and started long enough before bedtime, he would hear	190	_____
about Joseph the slave-boy, Joseph in prison, Joseph the dreamer,	200	_____
and Joseph the Big Man in Egypt.	207	_____

Needs Work   1   2   3   4   5   Excellent
Paid attention to punctuation

Needs Work   1   2   3   4   5   Excellent
Sounded good

Total Words Read _____

Total Errors − _____

Correct WPM _____

11
Fiction

from "The Life You Save May Be Your Own"
by Flannery O'Connor

	Words Read	Miscues

∞∞∞

The old woman and her daughter were sitting on their porch | 11 | _____
when Mr. Shiftlet came up their road for the first time. The old | 24 | _____
woman slid to the edge of her chair and leaned forward, shading | 36 | _____
her eyes from the piercing sunset with her hand. The daughter | 47 | _____
could not see far in front of her and continued to play with her | 61 | _____
fingers. Although the old woman lived in this desolate spot with | 72 | _____
only her daughter and she had never seen Mr. Shiftlet before, she | 84 | _____
could tell, even from a distance, that he was a tramp and no one | 98 | _____
to be afraid of. His left coat sleeve was folded up to show there | 112 | _____
was only half an arm in it and his gaunt figure listed slightly to | 126 | _____
the side as if the breeze were pushing him. He had on a black | 140 | _____
town suit and a brown felt hat that was turned up in the front | 154 | _____
and down in the back and he carried a tin tool box by a handle. | 169 | _____
He came on, at an amble, up her road, his face turned toward | 182 | _____
the sun which appeared to be balancing itself on the peak of a | 195 | _____
small mountain. | 197 | _____

Needs Work 1 2 3 4 5 Excellent
Paid attention to punctuation

Needs Work 1 2 3 4 5 Excellent
Sounded good

Total Words Read _____

Total Errors – _____

Correct WPM _____

11

Fiction

from **"The Life You Save May Be Your Own"**

by Flannery O'Connor

	Words Read	Miscues

The old woman and her daughter were sitting on their porch | 11 | _____ |
when Mr. Shiftlet came up their road for the first time. The old | 24 | _____ |
woman slid to the edge of her chair and leaned forward, shading | 36 | _____ |
her eyes from the piercing sunset with her hand. The daughter | 47 | _____ |
could not see far in front of her and continued to play with her | 61 | _____ |
fingers. Although the old woman lived in this desolate spot with | 72 | _____ |
only her daughter and she had never seen Mr. Shiftlet before, she | 84 | _____ |
could tell, even from a distance, that he was a tramp and no one | 98 | _____ |
to be afraid of. His left coat sleeve was folded up to show there | 112 | _____ |
was only half an arm in it and his gaunt figure listed slightly to | 126 | _____ |
the side as if the breeze were pushing him. He had on a black | 140 | _____ |
town suit and a brown felt hat that was turned up in the front | 154 | _____ |
and down in the back and he carried a tin tool box by a handle. | 169 | _____ |
He came on, at an amble, up her road, his face turned toward | 182 | _____ |
the sun which appeared to be balancing itself on the peak of a | 195 | _____ |
small mountain. | 197 | _____ |

Needs Work   1   2   3   4   5   Excellent
Paid attention to punctuation

Needs Work   1   2   3   4   5   Excellent
Sounded good

Total Words Read _____

Total Errors − _____

Correct WPM _____

12
Nonfiction

from *On the Way Home*
by Laura Ingalls Wilder and Rose Wilder Lane

First Reading

	Words Read	Miscues

How long [the] man worked with my father I don't remember.　11　_____
I cannot remember his name nor anything at all about his family　23　_____
camping down by the creek. Surely I knew those children; they　34　_____
must have been there for weeks. I remember that he and my　46　_____
father were roofing the little log barn, the day I chased the rabbit.　59　_____

The leaves had fallen from all the trees but the oaks then, and　72　_____
the oaks wore their winter red that day. There was light snow or　85　_____
frost underfoot, so cold that it burned my bare feet, and my　97　_____
breath puffed white in the air. I chased that rabbit over the hills,　110　_____
up and down and back again until, exhausted, it hid in a hollow　123　_____
log; I stopped up the log's ends with rocks and fetched both men　136　_____
from their work on the roof to chop out the rabbit and kill it.　150　_____

The day was Saturday; I was going to school then. For Sunday　162　_____
dinner we had rabbit stew, with gravy on mashed potatoes and on　174　_____
our cornbread. And on Monday I found in my lunch-pail at　185　_____
school one of that rabbit's legs; my mother had saved it and　197　_____
packed it with the cornbread in the little tin pail, to surprise me.　210　_____

Needs Work   1   2   3   4   5   Excellent
_____
Paid attention to punctuation

Needs Work   1   2   3   4   5   Excellent
_____
Sounded good

Total Words Read _____

Total Errors − _____

Correct WPM _____

12

Nonfiction

from *On the Way Home*
by Laura Ingalls Wilder and Rose Wilder Lane

	Words Read	Miscues

How long [the] man worked with my father I don't remember. `11` ———

I cannot remember his name nor anything at all about his family `23` ———

camping down by the creek. Surely I knew those children; they `34` ———

must have been there for weeks. I remember that he and my `46` ———

father were roofing the little log barn, the day I chased the rabbit. `59` ———

The leaves had fallen from all the trees but the oaks then, and `72` ———

the oaks wore their winter red that day. There was light snow or `85` ———

frost underfoot, so cold that it burned my bare feet, and my `97` ———

breath puffed white in the air. I chased that rabbit over the hills, `110` ———

up and down and back again until, exhausted, it hid in a hollow `123` ———

log; I stopped up the log's ends with rocks and fetched both men `136` ———

from their work on the roof to chop out the rabbit and kill it. `150` ———

The day was Saturday; I was going to school then. For Sunday `162` ———

dinner we had rabbit stew, with gravy on mashed potatoes and on `174` ———

our cornbread. And on Monday I found in my lunch-pail at `185` ———

school one of that rabbit's legs; my mother had saved it and `197` ———

packed it with the cornbread in the little tin pail, to surprise me. `210` ———

Needs Work 1 2 3 4 5 Excellent
Paid attention to punctuation

Needs Work 1 2 3 4 5 Excellent
Sounded good

Total Words Read ————

Total Errors – ————

Correct WPM ————

13

Nonfiction

from *Walt Whitman*
by Catherine Reef

	Words Read	Miscues

Walt Whitman found inspiration all around him. He wrote | 9 | _____
about the people he saw on his walks through New York City. He | 22 | _____
described the beaches of Long Island, where he was born, as well | 34 | _____
as that "Howler and scooper of storms," the sea. He celebrated the | 46 | _____
human body and explored his own complex human soul. "What a | 57 | _____
history is folded, folded inward and inward again," he wrote, "in | 68 | _____
the single word I." | 72 | _____

Today, the ferry ride inspired Whitman's imagination. He | 80 | _____
leaned against the rail and focused his pale eyes on the islands in | 93 | _____
New York Bay. He saw ships entering the harbor, ships flying the | 105 | _____
flags of far-off lands. A chilly wind rustled his gray beard as he | 118 | _____
turned toward the foundries on Brooklyn's shore. There, workers | 127 | _____
poured molten metal into molds to form tools and machine parts. | 138 | _____
In the twilight, their fires reflected yellow and red on the roofs of | 151 | _____
nearby houses. | 153 | _____

As he looked on these familiar scenes, Whitman thought about | 163 | _____
the many people who had also looked upon them. He thought | 174 | _____
about the many others, people not yet born, who would do so in | 187 | _____
the future. One hundred years later, those ferryboat passengers | 196 | _____
would share Whitman's experiences on that winter day. | 204 | _____

Needs Work   1 2 3 4 5   Excellent
Paid attention to punctuation

Needs Work   1 2 3 4 5   Excellent
Sounded good

Total Words Read _____

Total Errors − _____

Correct WPM _____

13

Nonfiction

from ***Walt Whitman***

by Catherine Reef

	Words Read	Miscues

Walt Whitman found inspiration all around him. He wrote about the people he saw on his walks through New York City. He described the beaches of Long Island, where he was born, as well as that "Howler and scooper of storms," the sea. He celebrated the human body and explored his own complex human soul. "What a history is folded, folded inward and inward again," he wrote, "in the single word I."

Today, the ferry ride inspired Whitman's imagination. He leaned against the rail and focused his pale eyes on the islands in New York Bay. He saw ships entering the harbor, ships flying the flags of far-off lands. A chilly wind rustled his gray beard as he turned toward the foundries on Brooklyn's shore. There, workers poured molten metal into molds to form tools and machine parts. In the twilight, their fires reflected yellow and red on the roofs of nearby houses.

As he looked on these familiar scenes, Whitman thought about the many people who had also looked upon them. He thought about the many others, people not yet born, who would do so in the future. One hundred years later, those ferryboat passengers would share Whitman's experiences on that winter day.

Words Read
9
22
34
46
57
68
72
80
93
105
118
127
138
151
153
163
174
187
196
204

Needs Work   1 2 3 4 5   Excellent
Paid attention to punctuation

Needs Work   1 2 3 4 5   Excellent
Sounded good

Total Words Read _____

Total Errors − _____

Correct WPM _____

14 Elephant Art

First Reading

	Words Read	Miscues

Ruby, an 8,000-pound Asian elephant at the Phoenix Zoo, is | 10 | _____
perhaps the best-known animal artist. Her paintings sell for | 19 | _____
$1,000 or more and hang in private collections beside the works | 30 | _____
of famous human artists. | 34 | _____

　　How did Ruby's keepers get the idea of letting her paint? | 45 | _____
Elephants have been observed using their trunks to draw in the | 56 | _____
dirt and marking the ground with twigs or rocks. Ruby had always | 68 | _____
doodled like this, so her keepers decided to give her art lessons. | 80 | _____
Within a week, Ruby was painting like a pro. | 89 | _____

　　Ruby is given a canvas and several choices of brushes and | 100 | _____
paints. An elephant's trunk contains 50,000 different muscles and | 109 | _____
can weigh as much as a man, but it can hold a paintbrush and use | 124 | _____
it delicately. With the tip of her trunk, Ruby points to the brush | 137 | _____
and color she wants. Her keeper dips the brush in the color of her | 151 | _____
choice and hands it to her. When a keeper tries to give her a color | 166 | _____
she has not selected, she refuses to use it. | 175 | _____

　　Where does an elephant get her ideas? Her keepers think that | 186 | _____
the red and blue that dominate one of Ruby's best known works, | 198 | _____
"Fire Truck," might have been inspired by emergency vehicles that | 208 | _____
arrived one day at the zoo to rescue a man. | 218 | _____

Needs Work　1　2　3　4　5　Excellent
Paid attention to punctuation

Needs Work　1　2　3　4　5　Excellent
Sounded good

Total Words Read _____

Total Errors − _____

Correct WPM _____

27

Elephant Art

	Words Read	Miscues

Ruby, an 8,000-pound Asian elephant at the Phoenix Zoo, is | 10 | _____

perhaps the best-known animal artist. Her paintings sell for | 19 | _____

$1,000 or more and hang in private collections beside the works | 30 | _____

of famous human artists. | 34 | _____

    How did Ruby's keepers get the idea of letting her paint? | 45 | _____

Elephants have been observed using their trunks to draw in the | 56 | _____

dirt and marking the ground with twigs or rocks. Ruby had always | 68 | _____

doodled like this, so her keepers decided to give her art lessons. | 80 | _____

Within a week, Ruby was painting like a pro. | 89 | _____

    Ruby is given a canvas and several choices of brushes and | 100 | _____

paints. An elephant's trunk contains 50,000 different muscles and | 109 | _____

can weigh as much as a man, but it can hold a paintbrush and use | 124 | _____

it delicately. With the tip of her trunk, Ruby points to the brush | 137 | _____

and color she wants. Her keeper dips the brush in the color of her | 151 | _____

choice and hands it to her. When a keeper tries to give her a color | 166 | _____

she has not selected, she refuses to use it. | 175 | _____

    Where does an elephant get her ideas? Her keepers think that | 186 | _____

the red and blue that dominate one of Ruby's best known works, | 198 | _____

"Fire Truck," might have been inspired by emergency vehicles that | 208 | _____

arrived one day at the zoo to rescue a man. | 218 | _____

Needs Work   1   2   3   4   5   Excellent
       Paid attention to punctuation

Needs Work   1   2   3   4   5   Excellent
       Sounded good

Total Words Read   _____

Total Errors   − _____

Correct WPM   _____

15 from *Dracula*
by Bram Stoker

Fiction

We pressed on the door, the rusty hinges creaked, and it slowly
opened. The Professor was the first to move forward, and stepped
into the open door. — **12, 23, 27**

We closed the door behind us, lest when we should have lit
our lamps we should possibly attract attention from the road. The
Professor carefully tried the lock, lest we might not be able to
open it from within should we be in a hurry making our exit.
Then we all lit our lamps and proceeded on our search. — **39, 50, 62, 75, 86**

The light from the tiny lamps fell in all sorts of odd forms, as
the rays crossed each other, or the opacity of our bodies threw
great shadows. I could not for my life get away from the feeling
that there was someone else amongst us. I think the feeling was
common to us all, for I noticed that the others kept looking over
their shoulders at every new shadow, just as I felt myself doing. — **100, 112, 125, 137, 150, 162**

The whole place was thick with dust. The floor was seemingly
inches deep, except where there were recent footsteps, in which
on holding down my lamp I could see marks of hobnails where
the dust was cracked. — **173, 183, 195, 199**

Words Read	Miscues
12	_____
23	_____
27	_____
39	_____
50	_____
62	_____
75	_____
86	_____
100	_____
112	_____
125	_____
137	_____
150	_____
162	_____
173	_____
183	_____
195	_____
199	_____

Needs Work   1   2   3   4   5   Excellent
Paid attention to punctuation

Needs Work   1   2   3   4   5   Excellent
Sounded good

Total Words Read _____

Total Errors − _____

Correct WPM _____

from *Dracula*

by Bram Stoker

	Words Read	Miscues
We pressed on the door, the rusty hinges creaked, and it slowly	12	_____
opened. The Professor was the first to move forward, and stepped	23	_____
into the open door.	27	_____
We closed the door behind us, lest when we should have lit	39	_____
our lamps we should possibly attract attention from the road. The	50	_____
Professor carefully tried the lock, lest we might not be able to	62	_____
open it from within should we be in a hurry making our exit.	75	_____
Then we all lit our lamps and proceeded on our search.	86	_____
The light from the tiny lamps fell in all sorts of odd forms, as	100	_____
the rays crossed each other, or the opacity of our bodies threw	112	_____
great shadows. I could not for my life get away from the feeling	125	_____
that there was someone else amongst us. I think the feeling was	137	_____
common to us all, for I noticed that the others kept looking over	150	_____
their shoulders at every new shadow, just as I felt myself doing.	162	_____
The whole place was thick with dust. The floor was seemingly	173	_____
inches deep, except where there were recent footsteps, in which	183	_____
on holding down my lamp I could see marks of hobnails where	195	_____
the dust was cracked.	199	_____

Needs Work 1 2 3 4 5 Excellent
Paid attention to punctuation

Needs Work 1 2 3 4 5 Excellent
Sounded good

Total Words Read _____

Total Errors − _____

Correct WPM _____

16 The Natural Wonders of Bryce Canyon

Nonfiction

	Words Read	Miscues

Caitlin and her mother arrived at Bryce Canyon National Park — 10

in Utah. — 12

"It's incredible, isn't it?" said Caitlin. "How was this canyon — 22

made?" — 23

"Well, according to this brochure," explained her mother, — 31

"millions of years of erosion created these rock formations. A — 41

huge lake formed here more than 100 million years ago and — 52

began wearing away the rock." She thumbed through her travel — 62

brochure. "It says here that the sediments carried and deposited — 72

by water became thousands of feet thick. The different minerals — 82

from the sediments created the variety of colors you see." — 92

Caitlin and her mother admired the smoky gray rocks at the — 103

base of the canyon. — 107

Her mother went on to explain, "It says in this brochure — 118

that Bryce Canyon isn't actually a canyon. It's a group of — 129

amphitheaters that have been carved by erosion. Amphitheaters — 137

are level areas that are surrounded by steep slopes." — 146

Some of the rock formations looked deep red or purple and — 157

blue in the setting sun. Her mother pointed to the Pink Cliffs. — 169

"The color in those rocks came from iron particles in the rocks — 181

that oxidized over time." — 185

Caitlin and her mother stood in awe of the spectacular display — 196

of color. — 198

Needs Work   1   2   3   4   5   Excellent
Paid attention to punctuation

Needs Work   1   2   3   4   5   Excellent
Sounded good

Total Words Read _____

Total Errors − _____

Correct WPM _____

31

The Natural Wonders of Bryce Canyon

	Words Read	Miscues

Caitlin and her mother arrived at Bryce Canyon National Park in Utah. — 10, 12

"It's incredible, isn't it?" said Caitlin. "How was this canyon made?" — 22, 23

"Well, according to this brochure," explained her mother, "millions of years of erosion created these rock formations. A huge lake formed here more than 100 million years ago and began wearing away the rock." She thumbed through her travel brochure. "It says here that the sediments carried and deposited by water became thousands of feet thick. The different minerals from the sediments created the variety of colors you see." — 31, 41, 52, 62, 72, 82, 92

Caitlin and her mother admired the smoky gray rocks at the base of the canyon. — 103, 107

Her mother went on to explain, "It says in this brochure that Bryce Canyon isn't actually a canyon. It's a group of amphitheaters that have been carved by erosion. Amphitheaters are level areas that are surrounded by steep slopes." — 118, 129, 137, 146

Some of the rock formations looked deep red or purple and blue in the setting sun. Her mother pointed to the Pink Cliffs. "The color in those rocks came from iron particles in the rocks that oxidized over time." — 157, 169, 181, 185

Caitlin and her mother stood in awe of the spectacular display of color. — 196, 198

Needs Work   1 2 3 4 5   Excellent
Paid attention to punctuation

Needs Work   1 2 3 4 5   Excellent
Sounded good

Total Words Read _____

Total Errors − _____

Correct WPM _____

17

Fiction

from "Dragon, Dragon"
by John Gardner

First Reading

	Words Read	Miscues

There was once a king whose kingdom was plagued by a
dragon. The king did not know which way to turn. The king's
knights were all cowards who hid under their beds whenever the
dragon came in sight, so they were of no use to the king at all.
And the king's wizard could not help either because, being old,
he had forgotten his magic spells. Nor could the wizard look up
the spells that had slipped his mind, for he had unfortunately
misplaced his wizard's book many years before. The king was
at his wit's end.

Every time there was a full moon the dragon came out of
his lair and ravaged the countryside. He frightened maidens
and stopped up chimneys and broke store windows and set
people's clocks back and made dogs bark until no one could hear
himself think.

He tipped over fences and robbed graves and put frogs in
people's drinking water and tore the last chapters out of novels
and changed house numbers around. . . .

He stole spark plugs out of people's cars and put firecrackers
in people's cigars and stole the clappers from all the church bells
and sprung every bear trap for miles around so the bears could
wander wherever they pleased.

Words Read
11
23
34
49
60
72
83
93
97
109
118
128
140
142
153
164
169
180
192
204
208

Needs Work   1   2   3   4   5   Excellent
Paid attention to punctuation

Needs Work   1   2   3   4   5   Excellent
Sounded good

Total Words Read _____

Total Errors − _____

Correct WPM _____

17 from **"Dragon, Dragon"**
by John Gardner

Fiction

	Words Read	Miscues

There was once a king whose kingdom was plagued by a   11 _____

dragon. The king did not know which way to turn. The king's   23 _____

knights were all cowards who hid under their beds whenever the   34 _____

dragon came in sight, so they were of no use to the king at all.   49 _____

And the king's wizard could not help either because, being old,   60 _____

he had forgotten his magic spells. Nor could the wizard look up   72 _____

the spells that had slipped his mind, for he had unfortunately   83 _____

misplaced his wizard's book many years before. The king was   93 _____

at his wit's end.   97 _____

Every time there was a full moon the dragon came out of   109 _____

his lair and ravaged the countryside. He frightened maidens   118 _____

and stopped up chimneys and broke store windows and set   128 _____

people's clocks back and made dogs bark until no one could hear   140 _____

himself think.   142 _____

He tipped over fences and robbed graves and put frogs in   153 _____

people's drinking water and tore the last chapters out of novels   164 _____

and changed house numbers around. . . .   169 _____

He stole spark plugs out of people's cars and put firecrackers   180 _____

in people's cigars and stole the clappers from all the church bells   192 _____

and sprung every bear trap for miles around so the bears could   204 _____

wander wherever they pleased.   208 _____

Needs Work   1   2   3   4   5   Excellent
Paid attention to punctuation

Needs Work   1   2   3   4   5   Excellent
Sounded good

Total Words Read _____

Total Errors −_____

Correct WPM _____

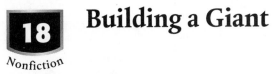

Building a Giant

Nonfiction

	Words Read	Miscues

As soon as his plan had been approved by the men who had   13 _____

sent him to America, the young sculptor, Frederic Auguste   22 _____

Bartholdi, started working on the designs of the Statue of Liberty.   33 _____

By 1875, he had already made several small study models.   43 _____

The most difficult problems were involved in the details of   53 _____

building. In solving them the sculptor had no guide but his own   65 _____

genius. The material must be light, easily worked, and of good   76 _____

appearance. It had to be strong enough to withstand the stress of   88 _____

a long ocean voyage. It had to withstand the effects of the salty   101 _____

air of New York Harbor. Copper was chosen as the material. The   113 _____

framework would be of iron and steel.   120 _____

To get the form of the statue, Bartholdi made a study model   132 _____

measuring about nine feet in height. Another model four times   142 _____

larger was made, giving the figure a height of 36 feet. This model   155 _____

was correct in every detail. Then the statue was divided into   166 _____

sections. Each of these was also made four times its size. These   178 _____

pieces, when joined together, formed the huge statue in its   188 _____

finished shape. The completed Statue of Liberty was officially   197 _____

dedicated on October 28, 1886.   202 _____

Needs Work   1 2 3 4 5   Excellent
Paid attention to punctuation

Needs Work   1 2 3 4 5   Excellent
Sounded good

Total Words Read _____

Total Errors − _____

Correct WPM _____

18 Nonfiction

Building a Giant

Second Reading

	Words Read	Miscues

As soon as his plan had been approved by the men who had   13 _____

sent him to America, the young sculptor, Frederic Auguste   22 _____

Bartholdi, started working on the designs of the Statue of Liberty.   33 _____

By 1875, he had already made several small study models.   43 _____

The most difficult problems were involved in the details of   53 _____

building. In solving them the sculptor had no guide but his own   65 _____

genius. The material must be light, easily worked, and of good   76 _____

appearance. It had to be strong enough to withstand the stress of   88 _____

a long ocean voyage. It had to withstand the effects of the salty   101 _____

air of New York Harbor. Copper was chosen as the material. The   113 _____

framework would be of iron and steel.   120 _____

To get the form of the statue, Bartholdi made a study model   132 _____

measuring about nine feet in height. Another model four times   142 _____

larger was made, giving the figure a height of 36 feet. This model   155 _____

was correct in every detail. Then the statue was divided into   166 _____

sections. Each of these was also made four times its size. These   178 _____

pieces, when joined together, formed the huge statue in its   188 _____

finished shape. The completed Statue of Liberty was officially   197 _____

dedicated on October 28, 1886.   202 _____

Needs Work   1   2   3   4   5   Excellent
Paid attention to punctuation

Needs Work   1   2   3   4   5   Excellent
Sounded good

Total Words Read   _____

Total Errors   – _____

Correct WPM   _____

19
Fiction

from *My Ántonia*
by Willa Cather

	Words Read	Miscues

If I loitered on the playground after school, or went to the   12   _____

post-office for the mail and lingered to hear the gossip about the   24   _____

cigar-stand, it would be growing dark by the time I came home.   36   _____

The sun was gone; the frozen streets stretched long and blue   47   _____

before me; the lights were shining pale in kitchen windows, and I   59   _____

could smell the suppers cooking as I passed. Few people were   70   _____

abroad, and each one of them was hurrying toward a fire. The   82   _____

glowing stoves in the houses were like magnets. When one passed   93   _____

an old man, one could see nothing of his face but a red nose   107   _____

sticking out between a frosted beard and a long plush cap. The   119   _____

young men capered along with their hands in their pockets, and   130   _____

sometimes tried a slide on the icy sidewalk. The children, in their   142   _____

bright hoods and comforters, never walked, but always ran from   152   _____

the moment they left their door, beating their mittens against   162   _____

their sides. When I got as far as the Methodist Church, I was   175   _____

about halfway home. I can remember how glad I was when there   187   _____

happened to be a light in the church, and the painted glass   199   _____

window shone out at us as we came along the frozen street.   211   _____

Needs Work   1   2   3   4   5   Excellent
Paid attention to punctuation

Needs Work   1   2   3   4   5   Excellent
Sounded good

Total Words Read   _____

Total Errors   − _____

Correct WPM   _____

19

Fiction

from *My Ántonia*

by Willa Cather

	Words Read	Miscues

If I loitered on the playground after school, or went to the | 12 | _____

post-office for the mail and lingered to hear the gossip about the | 24 | _____

cigar-stand, it would be growing dark by the time I came home. | 36 | _____

The sun was gone; the frozen streets stretched long and blue | 47 | _____

before me; the lights were shining pale in kitchen windows, and I | 59 | _____

could smell the suppers cooking as I passed. Few people were | 70 | _____

abroad, and each one of them was hurrying toward a fire. The | 82 | _____

glowing stoves in the houses were like magnets. When one passed | 93 | _____

an old man, one could see nothing of his face but a red nose | 107 | _____

sticking out between a frosted beard and a long plush cap. The | 119 | _____

young men capered along with their hands in their pockets, and | 130 | _____

sometimes tried a slide on the icy sidewalk. The children, in their | 142 | _____

bright hoods and comforters, never walked, but always ran from | 152 | _____

the moment they left their door, beating their mittens against | 162 | _____

their sides. When I got as far as the Methodist Church, I was | 175 | _____

about halfway home. I can remember how glad I was when there | 187 | _____

happened to be a light in the church, and the painted glass | 199 | _____

window shone out at us as we came along the frozen street. | 211 | _____

Needs Work   1   2   3   4   5   Excellent
Paid attention to punctuation

Needs Work   1   2   3   4   5   Excellent
Sounded good

Total Words Read _____

Total Errors − _____

Correct WPM _____

20

Nonfiction

from *A Brilliant Streak: The Making of Mark Twain*
by Kathryn Lasky

First Reading

	Words Read	Miscues

One autumn night more than a hundred and sixty years ago, a | 12 | _____
comet streaked across the sky over the tiny village of Florida, | 23 | _____
Missouri. That same night, in a clapboard cabin, Jane Lampton | 33 | _____
Clemens gave birth to her sixth child—Samuel Langhorne | 42 | _____
Clemens [Mark Twain]. He was premature and feeble. Jane and | 52 | _____
her husband, John, did not expect the baby to survive. | 62 | _____

The comet left a luminous glow long after it passed. Looking | 73 | _____
out the window, Jane Clemens might have felt that the comet was | 85 | _____
a sign, that there must be a link between the glorious fire in the | 99 | _____
sky and the tiny wrinkled baby she held in her arms on Earth. | 112 | _____

His parents hoped that Samuel would live through the night. | 122 | _____
He did. In fact, he lived until Halley's comet returned seventy-five | 133 | _____
years later. And between those two brilliant streaks in the sky, | 144 | _____
Samuel Langhorne Clemens lived enough lives for half a dozen | 154 | _____
other people as well. | 158 | _____

But there were many close calls. More than once—because of | 169 | _____
a combination of frail health and a mischievous nature—Sam had | 180 | _____
a close shave with death. If it wasn't measles or pneumonia, it was | 193 | _____
near-drownings. It is rumored that his parents became so used to | 204 | _____
sitting by his bed, waiting for him to die, they often fell asleep | 217 | _____
during the ordeal. | 220 | _____

Needs Work   1 2 3 4 5   Excellent
Paid attention to punctuation

Needs Work   1 2 3 4 5   Excellent
Sounded good

Total Words Read _____

Total Errors − _____

Correct WPM _____

from *A Brilliant Streak: The Making of Mark Twain*

by Kathryn Lasky

	Words Read	Miscues

One autumn night more than a hundred and sixty years ago, a — 12

comet streaked across the sky over the tiny village of Florida, — 23

Missouri. That same night, in a clapboard cabin, Jane Lampton — 33

Clemens gave birth to her sixth child—Samuel Langhorne — 42

Clemens [Mark Twain]. He was premature and feeble. Jane and — 52

her husband, John, did not expect the baby to survive. — 62

The comet left a luminous glow long after it passed. Looking — 73

out the window, Jane Clemens might have felt that the comet was — 85

a sign, that there must be a link between the glorious fire in the — 99

sky and the tiny wrinkled baby she held in her arms on Earth. — 112

His parents hoped that Samuel would live through the night. — 122

He did. In fact, he lived until Halley's comet returned seventy-five — 133

years later. And between those two brilliant streaks in the sky, — 144

Samuel Langhorne Clemens lived enough lives for half a dozen — 154

other people as well. — 158

But there were many close calls. More than once—because of — 169

a combination of frail health and a mischievous nature—Sam had — 180

a close shave with death. If it wasn't measles or pneumonia, it was — 193

near-drownings. It is rumored that his parents became so used to — 204

sitting by his bed, waiting for him to die, they often fell asleep — 217

during the ordeal. — 220

Needs Work   1   2   3   4   5   Excellent
Paid attention to punctuation

Needs Work   1   2   3   4   5   Excellent
Sounded good

Total Words Read _____

Total Errors − _____

Correct WPM _____

21

Fiction

from *Portrait of Jennie*
by Robert Nathan

	Words Read	Miscues

It was only then, as we started down the path to the shack, — 13

that I began to have an idea of what the wind was really like. Out — 28

there, on the water, I'd been too busy; and besides, in a sort of — 42

way, we had been part of it, moving with it, running before it. But — 56

here, facing the open sweep from the southeast, I caught it full — 68

and fair, and it hit me like a blow. — 77

The wind was coming across the Pamet in a steady flow, — 88

almost like a river of air in flood. There was no letup to it; it came — 104

flowing over heavy and solid and fast; it had pushed the marsh — 116

grass down flat, and bent the pines over in a quarter circle. There — 129

was something unnatural about it; it seemed to be coming from — 140

far away, but all the time it was coming nearer, and I had a feeling — 155

that it was darkness itself coming, and a force that didn't belong — 167

on this earth. My heart was beating fast; I felt cold and excited. I — 181

could hear that strange sound I had heard out on the bay, a sort — 195

of roaring hum, high up and far off; and the yellow-gray wall was — 208

still down there to the south. Or had it come closer? — 219

Needs Work   1 2 3 4 5   Excellent
Paid attention to punctuation

Needs Work   1 2 3 4 5   Excellent
Sounded good

Total Words Read _____

Total Errors − _____

Correct WPM _____

from *Portrait of Jennie*
by Robert Nathan

Second Reading

	Words Read	Miscues

It was only then, as we started down the path to the shack,   13

that I began to have an idea of what the wind was really like. Out   28

there, on the water, I'd been too busy; and besides, in a sort of   42

way, we had been part of it, moving with it, running before it. But   56

here, facing the open sweep from the southeast, I caught it full   68

and fair, and it hit me like a blow.   77

The wind was coming across the Pamet in a steady flow,   88

almost like a river of air in flood. There was no letup to it; it came   104

flowing over heavy and solid and fast; it had pushed the marsh   116

grass down flat, and bent the pines over in a quarter circle. There   129

was something unnatural about it; it seemed to be coming from   140

far away, but all the time it was coming nearer, and I had a feeling   155

that it was darkness itself coming, and a force that didn't belong   167

on this earth. My heart was beating fast; I felt cold and excited. I   181

could hear that strange sound I had heard out on the bay, a sort   195

of roaring hum, high up and far off; and the yellow-gray wall was   208

still down there to the south. Or had it come closer?   219

Needs Work   1 2 3 4 5 Excellent
Paid attention to punctuation

Needs Work   1 2 3 4 5 Excellent
Sounded good

Total Words Read   _____

Total Errors − _____

Correct WPM   _____

22

Nonfiction

from *China Homecoming*
by Jean Fritz

	Words Read	Miscues

When I was a child, my parents were always talking about   11   _____

"home." They meant America, of course, which sounded so   20   _____

wonderful I couldn't understand why they had ever left it. Why   31   _____

had they traveled halfway around the world to China to have me   43   _____

and then just stayed on, talking about "home"? Naturally, I   53   _____

wanted to hear about America but I could only daydream and   64   _____

wait for the years to go by until we would return. In the   77   _____

meantime my grandmother wrote me letters. She said she wished   87   _____

I was there to go blackberry picking with her. Or she told me she   101   _____

was baking an apple pie and why wasn't I around to peel the   114   _____

apples? I had never picked a blackberry in my life. I had never   127   _____

peeled an apple. Somehow, living on the opposite side of the   138   _____

world as I did, I didn't feel like a *real* American.   149   _____

But maybe when I was twelve years old, I told myself, I'd begin   162   _____

to feel like a real American. Twelve years old was the beginning of   175   _____

growing up, so perhaps I would change.   182   _____

The day before my twelfth birthday I asked my mother what   193   _____

the chances were, but, as usual, she was impatient with my   204   _____

American feelings.   206   _____

Needs Work   1   2   3   4   5   Excellent
Paid attention to punctuation

Needs Work   1   2   3   4   5   Excellent
Sounded good

Total Words Read   _____

Total Errors   – _____

Correct WPM   _____

22

Nonfiction

from *China Homecoming*

by Jean Fritz

When I was a child, my parents were always talking about "home." They meant America, of course, which sounded so wonderful I couldn't understand why they had ever left it. Why had they traveled halfway around the world to China to have me and then just stayed on, talking about "home"? Naturally, I wanted to hear about America but I could only daydream and wait for the years to go by until we would return. In the meantime my grandmother wrote me letters. She said she wished I was there to go blackberry picking with her. Or she told me she was baking an apple pie and why wasn't I around to peel the apples? I had never picked a blackberry in my life. I had never peeled an apple. Somehow, living on the opposite side of the world as I did, I didn't feel like a *real* American.

But maybe when I was twelve years old, I told myself, I'd begin to feel like a real American. Twelve years old was the beginning of growing up, so perhaps I would change.

The day before my twelfth birthday I asked my mother what the chances were, but, as usual, she was impatient with my American feelings.

11	_____
20	_____
31	_____
43	_____
53	_____
64	_____
77	_____
87	_____
101	_____
114	_____
127	_____
138	_____
149	_____
162	_____
175	_____
182	_____
193	_____
204	_____
206	_____

Needs Work   1   2   3   4   5   Excellent
Paid attention to punctuation

Needs Work   1   2   3   4   5   Excellent
Sounded good

Total Words Read _____

Total Errors − _____

Correct WPM _____

23

Fiction

from *To Kill a Mockingbird*
by Harper Lee

First Reading

	Words Read	Miscues

When he was nearly thirteen, my brother Jem got his arm
badly broken at the elbow. When it healed, and Jem's fears of
never being able to play football were assuaged, he was seldom
self-conscious about his injury. His left arm was somewhat shorter
than his right; when he stood or walked, the back of his hand was
at right angles to his body, his thumb parallel to his thigh. He
couldn't have cared less, so long as he could pass and punt.

When enough years had gone by to enable us to look back on
them, we sometimes discussed the events leading to his accident.
I maintain that the [Ewell family] started it all, but Jem, who was
four years my senior, said it started long before that. He said it
began the summer [our friend] Dill came to us, when Dill first
gave us the idea of making [our neighbor] Boo Radley come out.

I said if he wanted to take a broad view of the thing, it really
began with Andrew Jackson. If General Jackson hadn't run the
Creeks up the creek, Simon Finch would never have paddled up
the Alabama, and where would we be if he hadn't? We were far
too old to settle an argument with a fistfight, so we consulted
Atticus. Our father said we were both right.

Words Read
11
23
34
44
58
71
83
96
106
119
132
144
156
171
181
192
205
217
225

Needs Work   1   2   3   4   5   Excellent
Paid attention to punctuation

Needs Work   1   2   3   4   5   Excellent
Sounded good

Total Words Read _____

Total Errors − _____

Correct WPM _____

23

Fiction

from *To Kill a Mockingbird*
by Harper Lee

	Words Read	Miscues
When he was nearly thirteen, my brother Jem got his arm	11	_____
badly broken at the elbow. When it healed, and Jem's fears of	23	_____
never being able to play football were assuaged, he was seldom	34	_____
self-conscious about his injury. His left arm was somewhat shorter	44	_____
than his right; when he stood or walked, the back of his hand was	58	_____
at right angles to his body, his thumb parallel to his thigh. He	71	_____
couldn't have cared less, so long as he could pass and punt.	83	_____
When enough years had gone by to enable us to look back on	96	_____
them, we sometimes discussed the events leading to his accident.	106	_____
I maintain that the [Ewell family] started it all, but Jem, who was	119	_____
four years my senior, said it started long before that. He said it	132	_____
began the summer [our friend] Dill came to us, when Dill first	144	_____
gave us the idea of making [our neighbor] Boo Radley come out.	156	_____
I said if he wanted to take a broad view of the thing, it really	171	_____
began with Andrew Jackson. If General Jackson hadn't run the	181	_____
Creeks up the creek, Simon Finch would never have paddled up	192	_____
the Alabama, and where would we be if he hadn't? We were far	205	_____
too old to settle an argument with a fistfight, so we consulted	217	_____
Atticus. Our father said we were both right.	225	_____

Needs Work   1   2   3   4   5   Excellent
Paid attention to punctuation

Needs Work   1   2   3   4   5   Excellent
Sounded good

Total Words Read   _____

Total Errors   − _____

Correct WPM   _____

24 Heidi's Brush with Death

Nonfiction

	Words Read	Miscues

Heidi von Beltz had the world at her fingertips. As a teenager **12** _____
she was a superior athlete. Von Beltz was pretty enough to find **24** _____
work as a model. And since she loved to take on new physical **37** _____
challenges, she eventually became a Hollywood stuntwoman. **44** _____

In 1980, von Beltz was working in a film called *The Cannonball* **56** _____
Run with Burt Reynolds. One key scene called for von Beltz to be **69** _____
a passenger in a speeding car weaving through traffic. "We did it **81** _____
once," recalled von Beltz, "and it was fine." **89** _____

But the director wanted to try it again at higher speeds. This **101** _____
time it wasn't fine. The driver tried desperately to control the car, **113** _____
but the vehicle didn't respond quickly enough and the car **123** _____
slammed into a van. The force of the crash drove von Beltz into **136** _____
the dashboard and windshield, fracturing her spinal cord and **145** _____
smashing several neck vertebrae. **149** _____

Heidi von Beltz survived, but she was paralyzed from the neck **160** _____
down. Her doctors gave her five years to live. Instead, after years **172** _____
and years of therapy, she made a remarkable recovery, learning to **183** _____
sit up and stand by herself. **189** _____

This serious accident had a silver lining. The movie industry **199** _____
passed new rules regarding stunt safety. **205** _____

Needs Work   1   2   3   4   5   Excellent
Paid attention to punctuation

Needs Work   1   2   3   4   5   Excellent
Sounded good

Total Words Read _____

Total Errors − _____

Correct WPM _____

Heidi's Brush with Death

	Words Read	Miscues

Heidi von Beltz had the world at her fingertips. As a teenager she was a superior athlete. Von Beltz was pretty enough to find work as a model. And since she loved to take on new physical challenges, she eventually became a Hollywood stuntwoman.

In 1980, von Beltz was working in a film called *The Cannonball Run* with Burt Reynolds. One key scene called for von Beltz to be a passenger in a speeding car weaving through traffic. "We did it once," recalled von Beltz, "and it was fine."

But the director wanted to try it again at higher speeds. This time it wasn't fine. The driver tried desperately to control the car, but the vehicle didn't respond quickly enough and the car slammed into a van. The force of the crash drove von Beltz into the dashboard and windshield, fracturing her spinal cord and smashing several neck vertebrae.

Heidi von Beltz survived, but she was paralyzed from the neck down. Her doctors gave her five years to live. Instead, after years and years of therapy, she made a remarkable recovery, learning to sit up and stand by herself.

This serious accident had a silver lining. The movie industry passed new rules regarding stunt safety.

Words Read
12
24
37
44
56
69
81
89
101
113
123
136
145
149
160
172
183
189
199
205

Needs Work 1 2 3 4 5 Excellent
Paid attention to punctuation

Needs Work 1 2 3 4 5 Excellent
Sounded good

Total Words Read _____

Total Errors − _____

Correct WPM _____

25 from "The Medicine Bag"
by Virginia Driving Hawk Sneve

Fiction

First Reading

	Words Read	Miscues

⌇⌇⌇

My kid sister Cheryl and I always bragged about our Sioux	11	_____
grandpa, Joe Iron Shell. Our friends, who had always lived in the	23	_____
city and only knew about Indians from movies and TV, were	34	_____
impressed by our stories. Maybe we exaggerated and made	43	_____
Grandpa and the reservation sound glamorous, but when we'd	52	_____
return home to Iowa after our yearly summer visit to Grandpa	63	_____
we always had some exciting tale to tell.	71	_____
We always had some authentic Sioux article to show our	81	_____
listeners. One year Cheryl had new moccasins that Grandpa had	91	_____
made. On another visit he gave me a small, round, flat, rawhide	103	_____
drum which was decorated with a painting of a warrior riding a	115	_____
horse. He taught me a real Sioux chant to sing while I beat the	129	_____
drum with a leather-covered stick that had a feather on the end.	141	_____
Man, that really made an impression.	147	_____
We never showed our friends Grandpa's picture. Not that we	157	_____
were ashamed of him, but because we knew that the glamorous	168	_____
tales we told didn't go with the real thing. Our friends would have	181	_____
laughed at the picture, because Grandpa wasn't tall and stately	191	_____
like TV Indians. His hair wasn't in braids, but hung in stringy,	203	_____
gray strands on his neck and he was old.	212	_____

Needs Work   1   2   3   4   5   Excellent
Paid attention to punctuation

Needs Work   1   2   3   4   5   Excellent
Sounded good

Total Words Read _____

Total Errors – _____

Correct WPM _____

from "The Medicine Bag"
by Virginia Driving Hawk Sneve

	Words Read	Miscues

My kid sister Cheryl and I always bragged about our Sioux | 11 | _____
grandpa, Joe Iron Shell. Our friends, who had always lived in the | 23 | _____
city and only knew about Indians from movies and TV, were | 34 | _____
impressed by our stories. Maybe we exaggerated and made | 43 | _____
Grandpa and the reservation sound glamorous, but when we'd | 52 | _____
return home to Iowa after our yearly summer visit to Grandpa | 63 | _____
we always had some exciting tale to tell. | 71 | _____

We always had some authentic Sioux article to show our | 81 | _____
listeners. One year Cheryl had new moccasins that Grandpa had | 91 | _____
made. On another visit he gave me a small, round, flat, rawhide | 103 | _____
drum which was decorated with a painting of a warrior riding a | 115 | _____
horse. He taught me a real Sioux chant to sing while I beat the | 129 | _____
drum with a leather-covered stick that had a feather on the end. | 141 | _____
Man, that really made an impression. | 147 | _____

We never showed our friends Grandpa's picture. Not that we | 157 | _____
were ashamed of him, but because we knew that the glamorous | 168 | _____
tales we told didn't go with the real thing. Our friends would have | 181 | _____
laughed at the picture, because Grandpa wasn't tall and stately | 191 | _____
like TV Indians. His hair wasn't in braids, but hung in stringy, | 203 | _____
gray strands on his neck and he was old. | 212 | _____

Needs Work   1   2   3   4   5   Excellent
Paid attention to punctuation

Needs Work   1   2   3   4   5   Excellent
Sounded good

Total Words Read _____

Total Errors − _____

Correct WPM _____

26

Fiction

from "Broken Chain"
by Gary Soto

First Reading

	Words Read	Miscues

Alfonso didn't want to be the handsomest kid at school, but he   12   _____
was determined to be better-looking than average. The next day   22   _____
he spent his lawn-mowing money on a new shirt, and, with a   34   _____
pocketknife, scooped the moons of dirt from under his fingernails.   44   _____

He spent hours in front of the mirror trying to herd his teeth   57   _____
into place with his thumb. He asked his mother if he could have   70   _____
braces, like Frankie Molina, her godson, but he asked at the   81   _____
wrong time. She was at the kitchen table licking the envelope to   93   _____
the house payment. She glared up at him. "Do you think money   105   _____
grows on trees?"   108   _____

His mother clipped coupons from magazines and newspapers,   116   _____
kept a vegetable garden in the summer, and shopped at Penney's   127   _____
and K-Mart. Their family ate a lot of *frijoles,* which was OK   139   _____
because nothing else tasted so good, though one time Alfonso   149   _____
had had Chinese pot stickers and thought they were the next best   161   _____
food in the world.   165   _____

He didn't ask his mother for braces again, even when she was   177   _____
in a better mood. He decided to fix his teeth by pushing on them   191   _____
with his thumbs. After breakfast that Saturday he went to his   202   _____
room, closed the door quietly, turned the radio on, and pushed   213   _____
for three hours straight.   217   _____

Needs Work   1   2   3   4   5   Excellent
Paid attention to punctuation

Needs Work   1   2   3   4   5   Excellent
Sounded good

Total Words Read _____

Total Errors − _____

Correct WPM _____

26

Fiction

from "Broken Chain"
by Gary Soto

	Words Read	Miscues

Alfonso didn't want to be the handsomest kid at school, but he   12   _____
was determined to be better-looking than average. The next day   22   _____
he spent his lawn-mowing money on a new shirt, and, with a   34   _____
pocketknife, scooped the moons of dirt from under his fingernails.   44   _____

He spent hours in front of the mirror trying to herd his teeth   57   _____
into place with his thumb. He asked his mother if he could have   70   _____
braces, like Frankie Molina, her godson, but he asked at the   81   _____
wrong time. She was at the kitchen table licking the envelope to   93   _____
the house payment. She glared up at him. "Do you think money   105   _____
grows on trees?"   108   _____

His mother clipped coupons from magazines and newspapers,   116   _____
kept a vegetable garden in the summer, and shopped at Penney's   127   _____
and K-Mart. Their family ate a lot of *frijoles,* which was OK   139   _____
because nothing else tasted so good, though one time Alfonso   149   _____
had had Chinese pot stickers and thought they were the next best   161   _____
food in the world.   165   _____

He didn't ask his mother for braces again, even when she was   177   _____
in a better mood. He decided to fix his teeth by pushing on them   191   _____
with his thumbs. After breakfast that Saturday he went to his   202   _____
room, closed the door quietly, turned the radio on, and pushed   213   _____
for three hours straight.   217   _____

Needs Work   1   2   3   4   5   Excellent
Paid attention to punctuation

Needs Work   1   2   3   4   5   Excellent
Sounded good

Total Words Read   _____

Total Errors – _____

Correct WPM   _____

27
Nonfiction

from "A Christmas Memory"
by Truman Capote

	Words Read	Miscues

	Words Read	Miscues
Having stuffed our burlap sacks with enough greenery and	9	_____
crimson to garland a dozen windows, we set about choosing a	20	_____
tree. "It should be," muses my friend, "twice as tall as a boy. So	34	_____
a boy can't steal the star." The one we pick is twice as tall as me.	50	_____
A brave handsome brute that survives thirty hatchet strokes	59	_____
before it keels with a creaking rending cry. Lugging it like a kill,	72	_____
we commence the long trek out. Every few yards we abandon the	84	_____
struggle, sit down and pant. But we have the strength of	95	_____
triumphant huntsmen; that and the tree's virile, icy perfume	104	_____
revive us, goad us on. Many compliments accompany our sunset	114	_____
return along the red clay road to town; but my friend is sly and	128	_____
noncommittal when passers-by praise the treasure perched in	136	_____
our buggy: what a fine tree and where did it come from?	148	_____
"Yonderways," she murmurs vaguely. Once a car stops and the	158	_____
rich mill owner's lazy wife leans out and whines: "Giveya two-bits	169	_____
cash for that ol tree." Ordinarily my friend is afraid of saying no;	182	_____
but on this occasion she promptly shakes her head: "We wouldn't	193	_____
take a dollar."	196	_____

Needs Work   1 2 3 4 5   Excellent
Paid attention to punctuation

Needs Work   1 2 3 4 5   Excellent
Sounded good

Total Words Read _____

Total Errors − _____

Correct WPM _____

from **"A Christmas Memory"**

by Truman Capote

	Words Read	Miscues
Having stuffed our burlap sacks with enough greenery and	9	_____
crimson to garland a dozen windows, we set about choosing a	20	_____
tree. "It should be," muses my friend, "twice as tall as a boy. So	34	_____
a boy can't steal the star." The one we pick is twice as tall as me.	50	_____
A brave handsome brute that survives thirty hatchet strokes	59	_____
before it keels with a creaking rending cry. Lugging it like a kill,	72	_____
we commence the long trek out. Every few yards we abandon the	84	_____
struggle, sit down and pant. But we have the strength of	95	_____
triumphant huntsmen; that and the tree's virile, icy perfume	104	_____
revive us, goad us on. Many compliments accompany our sunset	114	_____
return along the red clay road to town; but my friend is sly and	128	_____
noncommittal when passers-by praise the treasure perched in	136	_____
our buggy: what a fine tree and where did it come from?	148	_____
"Yonderways," she murmurs vaguely. Once a car stops and the	158	_____
rich mill owner's lazy wife leans out and whines: "Giveya two-bits	169	_____
cash for that ol tree." Ordinarily my friend is afraid of saying no;	182	_____
but on this occasion she promptly shakes her head: "We wouldn't	193	_____
take a dollar."	196	_____

Needs Work 1 2 3 4 5 Excellent
Paid attention to punctuation

Needs Work 1 2 3 4 5 Excellent
Sounded good

Total Words Read _____

Total Errors – _____

Correct WPM _____

Cristina Sanchez, Bullfighter

First Reading

	Words Read	Miscues

28
Nonfiction

Text	Words Read	Miscues
Cristina Sanchez's dream was to do just what her father had	11	_____
done. Like him, she wanted to be a matador and fight fierce bulls	24	_____
to the cheers of adoring fans. But Antonio Sanchez didn't want	35	_____
his young daughter to be a bullfighter. The bullring, he told her,	47	_____
was far too dangerous and besides, it was no place for a girl.	60	_____
Still, Cristina Sanchez willingly took on the dangers and the	70	_____
prejudice. She graduated first in her class at the bullfighting	80	_____
school in Madrid. Slowly, she worked her way up through the	91	_____
bush leagues of bullfighting. She began by fighting two-year-old	100	_____
bulls in small rinks. Then she moved on to three-year-old bulls in	112	_____
larger arenas. It wasn't easy. Even small bulls can be dangerous.	123	_____
Three times they gored her seriously, twice in her right thigh and	135	_____
once in her stomach.	139	_____
And then there were the ever-present loudmouths. Despite her	148	_____
grace and showmanship, Cristina was taunted by spectators.	156	_____
At last, on May 25, 1996, Cristina Sanchez made it to the	168	_____
major leagues of bullfighting. She faced and defeated a fully-	178	_____
grown four-year-old bull. Even the most macho of Spanish men	187	_____
had to admit she was good. Cristina quickly became a fan favorite,	199	_____
earning more than a million dollars a year.	207	_____
Today, she is at the top of her sport.	216	_____

Needs Work 1 2 3 4 5 Excellent
Paid attention to punctuation

Needs Work 1 2 3 4 5 Excellent
Sounded good

Total Words Read _____

Total Errors − _____

Correct WPM _____

Cristina Sanchez, Bullfighter

	Words Read	Miscues

Cristina Sanchez's dream was to do just what her father had — 11

done. Like him, she wanted to be a matador and fight fierce bulls — 24

to the cheers of adoring fans. But Antonio Sanchez didn't want — 35

his young daughter to be a bullfighter. The bullring, he told her, — 47

was far too dangerous and besides, it was no place for a girl. — 60

Still, Cristina Sanchez willingly took on the dangers and the — 70

prejudice. She graduated first in her class at the bullfighting — 80

school in Madrid. Slowly, she worked her way up through the — 91

bush leagues of bullfighting. She began by fighting two-year-old — 100

bulls in small rinks. Then she moved on to three-year-old bulls in — 112

larger arenas. It wasn't easy. Even small bulls can be dangerous. — 123

Three times they gored her seriously, twice in her right thigh and — 135

once in her stomach. — 139

And then there were the ever-present loudmouths. Despite her — 148

grace and showmanship, Cristina was taunted by spectators. — 156

At last, on May 25, 1996, Cristina Sanchez made it to the — 168

major leagues of bullfighting. She faced and defeated a fully- — 178

grown four-year-old bull. Even the most macho of Spanish men — 187

had to admit she was good. Cristina quickly became a fan favorite, — 199

earning more than a million dollars a year. — 207

Today, she is at the top of her sport. — 216

Needs Work   1   2   3   4   5   Excellent
Paid attention to punctuation

Needs Work   1   2   3   4   5   Excellent
Sounded good

Total Words Read _____

Total Errors − _____

Correct WPM _____

29

Fiction

from **"Two Kinds"**

by Amy Tan

	Words Read	Miscues

Every night after dinner my mother and I would sit at the | 12 | _____

Formica-topped kitchen table. She would present new tests, taking | 21 | _____

her examples from stories of amazing children that she had read | 32 | _____

in *Ripley's Believe It or Not* or *Good Housekeeping, Reader's Digest,* | 43 | _____

or any of a dozen other magazines she kept in a pile in our | 57 | _____

bathroom. My mother got these magazines from people whose | 66 | _____

houses she cleaned. And since she cleaned many houses each | 76 | _____

week, we had a great assortment. She would look through them | 87 | _____

all, searching for stories about remarkable children. | 94 | _____

The first night she brought out a story about a three-year-old | 105 | _____

boy who knew the capitals of all the states and even of most of | 119 | _____

the European countries. A teacher was quoted as saying that the | 130 | _____

little boy could also pronounce the names of the foreign cities | 141 | _____

correctly. "What's the capital of Finland?" my mother asked me, | 151 | _____

looking at the story. | 155 | _____

All I knew was the capital of California, because Sacramento | 165 | _____

was the name of the street we lived on in Chinatown. "Nairobi!" | 177 | _____

I guessed, saying the most foreign word I could think of. She | 189 | _____

checked to see if that might be one way to pronounce *Helsinki* | 201 | _____

before showing me the answer. | 206 | _____

Needs Work   1   2   3   4   5   Excellent
Paid attention to punctuation

Needs Work   1   2   3   4   5   Excellent
Sounded good

Total Words Read _____

Total Errors − _____

Correct WPM _____

from **"Two Kinds"**

by Amy Tan

	Words Read	Miscues

Every night after dinner my mother and I would sit at the | 12 | _____

Formica-topped kitchen table. She would present new tests, taking | 21 | _____

her examples from stories of amazing children that she had read | 32 | _____

in *Ripley's Believe It or Not* or *Good Housekeeping, Reader's Digest,* | 43 | _____

or any of a dozen other magazines she kept in a pile in our | 57 | _____

bathroom. My mother got these magazines from people whose | 66 | _____

houses she cleaned. And since she cleaned many houses each | 76 | _____

week, we had a great assortment. She would look through them | 87 | _____

all, searching for stories about remarkable children. | 94 | _____

The first night she brought out a story about a three-year-old | 105 | _____

boy who knew the capitals of all the states and even of most of | 119 | _____

the European countries. A teacher was quoted as saying that the | 130 | _____

little boy could also pronounce the names of the foreign cities | 141 | _____

correctly. "What's the capital of Finland?" my mother asked me, | 151 | _____

looking at the story. | 155 | _____

All I knew was the capital of California, because Sacramento | 165 | _____

was the name of the street we lived on in Chinatown. "Nairobi!" | 177 | _____

I guessed, saying the most foreign word I could think of. She | 189 | _____

checked to see if that might be one way to pronounce *Helsinki* | 201 | _____

before showing me the answer. | 206 | _____

Needs Work   1   2   3   4   5   Excellent
Paid attention to punctuation

Needs Work   1   2   3   4   5   Excellent
Sounded good

Total Words Read _____

Total Errors − _____

Correct WPM _____

30

Nonfiction

from *When Plague Strikes*
by James Cross Giblin

First Reading

	Words Read	Miscues

Within weeks of the first reported cases [of plague], hundreds — 10 — _____
of people in the Black Sea region had sickened and died. Those — 22 — _____
who survived were terrified. They had no medicines with which to — 33 — _____
fight the disease. As it continued to spread, their fear changed to — 45 — _____
frustration, and then to anger. Someone—some outsider—must — 54 — _____
be responsible for bringing this calamity upon them. — 62 — _____

The most likely candidates were the Italian traders who — 71 — _____
operated in the region. They bartered Italian goods for the silks — 82 — _____
and spices that came over the caravan routes from the Far East, — 94 — _____
then shipped the Eastern merchandise on to Italy. Although many — 104 — _____
of the traders had lived in the region for years, they were still — 117 — _____
thought of as being different. For one thing, they were Christians, — 128 — _____
while most of the natives were Muslims. — 135 — _____

Deciding the Italians were to blame for the epidemic, the — 145 — _____
natives gathered an army and prepared to attack their trading — 155 — _____
post. The Italians fled to a fortress they had built on the coast of — 169 — _____
the Black Sea. There the natives besieged them until the dread — 180 — _____
disease broke out in the Muslim army. — 187 — _____

The natives were forced to withdraw. But before they did— — 197 — _____
according to one account—they gave the Italians a taste of the — 209 — _____
agony their people had been suffering. — 215 — _____

Needs Work   1 2 3 4 5   Excellent
Paid attention to punctuation

Needs Work   1 2 3 4 5   Excellent
Sounded good

Total Words Read   _____

Total Errors   − _____

Correct WPM   _____

from *When Plague Strikes*
by James Cross Giblin

❦

	Words Read	Miscues

Within weeks of the first reported cases [of plague], hundreds — **10**

of people in the Black Sea region had sickened and died. Those — **22**

who survived were terrified. They had no medicines with which to — **33**

fight the disease. As it continued to spread, their fear changed to — **45**

frustration, and then to anger. Someone—some outsider—must — **54**

be responsible for bringing this calamity upon them. — **62**

The most likely candidates were the Italian traders who — **71**

operated in the region. They bartered Italian goods for the silks — **82**

and spices that came over the caravan routes from the Far East, — **94**

then shipped the Eastern merchandise on to Italy. Although many — **104**

of the traders had lived in the region for years, they were still — **117**

thought of as being different. For one thing, they were Christians, — **128**

while most of the natives were Muslims. — **135**

Deciding the Italians were to blame for the epidemic, the — **145**

natives gathered an army and prepared to attack their trading — **155**

post. The Italians fled to a fortress they had built on the coast of — **169**

the Black Sea. There the natives besieged them until the dread — **180**

disease broke out in the Muslim army. — **187**

The natives were forced to withdraw. But before they did— — **197**

according to one account—they gave the Italians a taste of the — **209**

agony their people had been suffering. — **215**

Needs Work   1 2 3 4 5   Excellent
Paid attention to punctuation

Needs Work   1 2 3 4 5   Excellent
Sounded good

Total Words Read _____

Total Errors − _____

Correct WPM _____

31
Fiction

The Spirit Plate

	Words Read	Miscues

Once a week my mother and I walk to the cemetery with food | 13 | _____

for my grandmother and other relatives who have died. We bring | 24 | _____

a little meat and bread, soup, and sometimes a jar of hot coffee to | 38 | _____

place near the graves. | 42 | _____

First we clean the gravestones and the area all around them. | 53 | _____

We sweep off the soil the wind has blown over them, and we pull | 67 | _____

out weeds that have grown there. Then we sing the old honoring | 79 | _____

songs and memorial songs of our Lakota people. These songs | 89 | _____

have been passed down from person to person for many | 99 | _____

generations. My mother told me how her grandmother used to | 109 | _____

sing these songs whenever the soldiers came through our | 118 | _____

reservation. Everyone was proud of how brave she was! | 127 | _____

In addition to placing food at our ancestors' graves, we honor | 138 | _____

the spirits of our ancestors at every main meal by setting a spirit | 151 | _____

plate for them. We take one plate, bless it, and fill it with a tiny | 166 | _____

bit of every food at the meal. Then we place the plate near the | 180 | _____

center of the table and pray over it before anyone eats. I never | 193 | _____

see anything disappear from the plate, but I know that the good | 205 | _____

spirits of my ancestors are eating the energy of the food. They | 217 | _____

know that they are remembered and celebrated. | 224 | _____

Needs Work   1   2   3   4   5   Excellent
Paid attention to punctuation

Needs Work   1   2   3   4   5   Excellent
Sounded good

Total Words Read _____

Total Errors − _____

Correct WPM _____

61

31

Fiction

The Spirit Plate

	Words Read	Miscues

Once a week my mother and I walk to the cemetery with food | 13 | _____
for my grandmother and other relatives who have died. We bring | 24 | _____
a little meat and bread, soup, and sometimes a jar of hot coffee to | 38 | _____
place near the graves. | 42 | _____

First we clean the gravestones and the area all around them. | 53 | _____
We sweep off the soil the wind has blown over them, and we pull | 67 | _____
out weeds that have grown there. Then we sing the old honoring | 79 | _____
songs and memorial songs of our Lakota people. These songs | 89 | _____
have been passed down from person to person for many | 99 | _____
generations. My mother told me how her grandmother used to | 109 | _____
sing these songs whenever the soldiers came through our | 118 | _____
reservation. Everyone was proud of how brave she was! | 127 | _____

In addition to placing food at our ancestors' graves, we honor | 138 | _____
the spirits of our ancestors at every main meal by setting a spirit | 151 | _____
plate for them. We take one plate, bless it, and fill it with a tiny | 166 | _____
bit of every food at the meal. Then we place the plate near the | 180 | _____
center of the table and pray over it before anyone eats. I never | 193 | _____
see anything disappear from the plate, but I know that the good | 205 | _____
spirits of my ancestors are eating the energy of the food. They | 217 | _____
know that they are remembered and celebrated. | 224 | _____

Needs Work   1   2   3   4   5   Excellent
Paid attention to punctuation

Needs Work   1   2   3   4   5   Excellent
Sounded good

Total Words Read _____

Total Errors − _____

Correct WPM _____

32 from "A Crush"
Fiction

by Cynthia Rylant

	Words Read	Miscues

It was 6:00 A.M. and the building was still dark. Ernie set the clear · 14 · _____

mason jar full of flowers under the sign that read "Closed," then · 26 · _____

he smiled at Jack and followed him back across the street to · 38 · _____

get breakfast. · 40 · _____

When Dolores arrived at seven and picked up the jar of zinnias · 52 · _____

and cornflowers and nasturtiums and marigolds and asters and · 61 · _____

four-o'clocks, Ernie and Jack were watching her from a booth in · 72 · _____

the Big Boy. Each had a wide smile on his face as Dolores put · 86 · _____

her nose to the flowers. Ernie giggled. They watched the lights of · 98 · _____

the hardware store come up and saw Dolores place the clear · 109 · _____

mason jar on the ledge of the front window. They drove home · 121 · _____

still smiling. · 123 · _____

All the rest of that summer Ernie left a jar of flowers every · 136 · _____

Wednesday morning at the front door of Stan's Hardware. Neither · 146 · _____

Dick Wilcox nor Dolores could figure out why the flowers kept · 157 · _____

coming, and each of them assumed somebody had a crush on the · 169 · _____

other. But the flowers had an effect on them anyway. Dick started · 181 · _____

spending more time out on the floor making conversation with · 191 · _____

the customers, while Dolores stopped wearing T-shirts to work · 200 · _____

and instead wore crisp white blouses with the sleeves rolled back · 211 · _____

off her wrists. · 214 · _____

Needs Work   1 2 3 4 5   Excellent
Paid attention to punctuation

Needs Work   1 2 3 4 5   Excellent
Sounded good

Total Words Read _____

Total Errors − _____

Correct WPM _____

from "A Crush"

by Cynthia Rylant

	Words Read	Miscues

It was 6:00 A.M. and the building was still dark. Ernie set the clear — 14

mason jar full of flowers under the sign that read "Closed," then — 26

he smiled at Jack and followed him back across the street to — 38

get breakfast. — 40

When Dolores arrived at seven and picked up the jar of zinnias — 52

and cornflowers and nasturtiums and marigolds and asters and — 61

four-o'clocks, Ernie and Jack were watching her from a booth in — 72

the Big Boy. Each had a wide smile on his face as Dolores put — 86

her nose to the flowers. Ernie giggled. They watched the lights of — 98

the hardware store come up and saw Dolores place the clear — 109

mason jar on the ledge of the front window. They drove home — 121

still smiling. — 123

All the rest of that summer Ernie left a jar of flowers every — 136

Wednesday morning at the front door of Stan's Hardware. Neither — 146

Dick Wilcox nor Dolores could figure out why the flowers kept — 157

coming, and each of them assumed somebody had a crush on the — 169

other. But the flowers had an effect on them anyway. Dick started — 181

spending more time out on the floor making conversation with — 191

the customers, while Dolores stopped wearing T-shirts to work — 200

and instead wore crisp white blouses with the sleeves rolled back — 211

off her wrists. — 214

Needs Work   1   2   3   4   5   Excellent
Paid attention to punctuation

Needs Work   1   2   3   4   5   Excellent
Sounded good

Total Words Read _____

Total Errors − _____

Correct WPM _____

33 from "Satchel Paige"

Nonfiction

by Bill Littlefield

	Words Read	Miscues

The tall, skinny kid named Leroy Paige became Satchel Paige   10 _____

one day at the railroad station in Mobile, Alabama. He was   21 _____

carrying bags for the folks getting on and off the trains, earning   33 _____

all the nickels and dimes he could to help feed his ten brothers   46 _____

and sisters. Eventually it occurred to him that if he slung a pole   59 _____

across his narrow shoulders and hung the bags, or satchels, on the   71 _____

ends of the pole, he could carry for more people at once and   84 _____

collect more nickels and dimes. It worked, but it looked a little   96 _____

funny. "You look like some kind of ol' satchel tree," one of his   109 _____

friends told him, and the nickname stuck.   116 _____

Even in those days, before he was a teenager, Satchel Paige   127 _____

could throw hard and accurately. Years later, Paige swore that   137 _____

when his mother would send him out into the yard to get a   150 _____

chicken for dinner, he would brain the bird with a rock. "I used   163 _____

to kill *flying* birds with rocks, too," he said. "Most people need   175 _____

shotguns to do what I did with rocks."   183 _____

It was not a talent that would go unnoticed for long.   194 _____

Needs Work   1   2   3   4   5   Excellent
   Paid attention to punctuation

Needs Work   1   2   3   4   5   Excellent
   Sounded good

Total Words Read _____

Total Errors − _____

Correct WPM _____

from "Satchel Paige"

by Bill Littlefield

	Words Read	Miscues

The tall, skinny kid named Leroy Paige became Satchel Paige   10   _____
one day at the railroad station in Mobile, Alabama. He was   21   _____
carrying bags for the folks getting on and off the trains, earning   33   _____
all the nickels and dimes he could to help feed his ten brothers   46   _____
and sisters. Eventually it occurred to him that if he slung a pole   59   _____
across his narrow shoulders and hung the bags, or satchels, on the   71   _____
ends of the pole, he could carry for more people at once and   84   _____
collect more nickels and dimes. It worked, but it looked a little   96   _____
funny. "You look like some kind of ol' satchel tree," one of his   109   _____
friends told him, and the nickname stuck.   116   _____

Even in those days, before he was a teenager, Satchel Paige   127   _____
could throw hard and accurately. Years later, Paige swore that   137   _____
when his mother would send him out into the yard to get a   150   _____
chicken for dinner, he would brain the bird with a rock. "I used   163   _____
to kill *flying* birds with rocks, too," he said. "Most people need   175   _____
shotguns to do what I did with rocks."   183   _____

It was not a talent that would go unnoticed for long.   194   _____

Needs Work   1   2   3   4   5   Excellent
Paid attention to punctuation

Needs Work   1   2   3   4   5   Excellent
Sounded good

Total Words Read   _____

Total Errors   − _____

Correct WPM   _____

34

Fiction

from **"The Flat of the Land"**
by Diana Garcia

	Words Read	Miscues

In the predawn hours, Amparo awoke to the lurch of the | 11 | _____
house lifting and settling on a wide river of mud. House and | 23 | _____
mud paused as she clambered to the roof. They allowed her time | 35 | _____
to adjust her stance to the house's uncommon roll, then the | 46 | _____
house made a slow 180-degree turn from the old highway to | 57 | _____
the foothills. | 59 | _____

Like a swimmer learning a new stroke, the house muscled | 69 | _____
through the mud, at first tentatively, then with increased fluidity. | 79 | _____
Loose pieces of masonry scattered as the house and mud picked | 90 | _____
up speed. The mud wash kicked up nearly one story high, | 101 | _____
flattening sage and manzanita. | 105 | _____

"We're coming, we're coming, it won't be long before we're | 115 | _____
there," Amparo shouted to the hills. To the sun she complained, | 126 | _____
"We need some light over here. How do you expect us to see | 139 | _____
where we're going if you wait until six o'clock to get up?" To the | 153 | _____
house and mud she instructed, "Faster, go faster, we're almost | 163 | _____
there! Don't worry about me." As they drew closer, a cleft in the | 176 | _____
foothills parted, and house, mud, woman squeezed through in an | 186 | _____
eruption of closely contained forms, aiming for the tree-laced | 195 | _____
meadow above. | 197 | _____

Needs Work   1   2   3   4   5   Excellent
Paid attention to punctuation

Needs Work   1   2   3   4   5   Excellent
Sounded good

Total Words Read _____

Total Errors − _____

Correct WPM _____

34

Fiction

from **"The Flat of the Land"**

by Diana Garcia

	Words Read	Miscues

In the predawn hours, Amparo awoke to the lurch of the house lifting and settling on a wide river of mud. House and mud paused as she clambered to the roof. They allowed her time to adjust her stance to the house's uncommon roll, then the house made a slow 180-degree turn from the old highway to the foothills.

Like a swimmer learning a new stroke, the house muscled through the mud, at first tentatively, then with increased fluidity. Loose pieces of masonry scattered as the house and mud picked up speed. The mud wash kicked up nearly one story high, flattening sage and manzanita.

"We're coming, we're coming, it won't be long before we're there," Amparo shouted to the hills. To the sun she complained, "We need some light over here. How do you expect us to see where we're going if you wait until six o'clock to get up?" To the house and mud she instructed, "Faster, go faster, we're almost there! Don't worry about me." As they drew closer, a cleft in the foothills parted, and house, mud, woman squeezed through in an eruption of closely contained forms, aiming for the tree-laced meadow above.

Words Read
11
23
35
46
57
59
69
79
90
101
105
115
126
139
153
163
176
186
195
197

Needs Work   1   2   3   4   5   Excellent
Paid attention to punctuation

Needs Work   1   2   3   4   5   Excellent
Sounded good

Total Words Read _____

Total Errors − _____

Correct WPM _____

The Florida Skunk Ape

35

Nonfiction

	Words Read	Miscues

It was a cool February night in 1970. H. C. "Buz" Osborn and — 13 _____

four companions were sleeping peacefully in their tents. They — 22 _____

were all worn out after a day spent studying a Native American — 34 _____

burial ground in southern Florida. Suddenly, at 3 A.M., a noise — 45 _____

woke them. Looking up, they saw a strange eight-foot creature — 55 _____

standing just outside the flap doors of their tents. It was covered — 67 _____

with hair and, according to one of the men, "smelled awful." But — 79 _____

the creature did not harm the men, and soon it disappeared into — 91 _____

the dark night. — 94 _____

In the morning, the campers found five-toed footprints around — 103 _____

their tent. The prints were $17\frac{1}{2}$ inches long and 11 inches wide. — 115 _____

They must have been made by the massive creature the men had — 127 _____

seen the night before. Osborn was a no-nonsense kind of guy. An — 139 _____

engineer and amateur archaeologist, he had never believed in the — 149 _____

Florida legend about a Skunk Ape living in the remote regions of — 161 _____

the Everglades. But, Osborn said, the visitor early that morning — 171 _____

and the prints it left behind "made a believer out of me." — 183 _____

Osborn and his friends haven't been the only people to notice — 194 _____

this odd creature. Since the 1920s, there have been numerous — 204 _____

sightings of the so-called Florida Skunk Ape. — 211 _____

Needs Work   1   2   3   4   5   Excellent
Paid attention to punctuation

Needs Work   1   2   3   4   5   Excellent
Sounded good

Total Words Read _____

Total Errors − _____

Correct WPM _____

The Florida Skunk Ape

	Words Read	Miscues
It was a cool February night in 1970. H. C. "Buz" Osborn and	13	_____
four companions were sleeping peacefully in their tents. They	22	_____
were all worn out after a day spent studying a Native American	34	_____
burial ground in southern Florida. Suddenly, at 3 A.M., a noise	45	_____
woke them. Looking up, they saw a strange eight-foot creature	55	_____
standing just outside the flap doors of their tents. It was covered	67	_____
with hair and, according to one of the men, "smelled awful." But	79	_____
the creature did not harm the men, and soon it disappeared into	91	_____
the dark night.	94	_____
In the morning, the campers found five-toed footprints around	103	_____
their tent. The prints were 17½ inches long and 11 inches wide.	115	_____
They must have been made by the massive creature the men had	127	_____
seen the night before. Osborn was a no-nonsense kind of guy. An	139	_____
engineer and amateur archaeologist, he had never believed in the	149	_____
Florida legend about a Skunk Ape living in the remote regions of	161	_____
the Everglades. But, Osborn said, the visitor early that morning	171	_____
and the prints it left behind "made a believer out of me."	183	_____
Osborn and his friends haven't been the only people to notice	194	_____
this odd creature. Since the 1920s, there have been numerous	204	_____
sightings of the so-called Florida Skunk Ape.	211	_____

Needs Work 1 2 3 4 5 Excellent
Paid attention to punctuation

Needs Work 1 2 3 4 5 Excellent
Sounded good

Total Words Read _____

Total Errors − _____

Correct WPM _____

36

Fiction

from *The Jungle Books*
by Rudyard Kipling

First Reading

	Words Read	Miscues

Sea Catch was fifteen years old, a huge gray fur seal with almost   13   _____

a mane on his shoulders, and long, wicked dogteeth. When he   24   _____

heaved himself up on his front flippers he stood more than four   36   _____

feet clear of the ground. His weight, if anyone had been bold   48   _____

enough to weigh him, was nearly seven hundred pounds. He was   59   _____

scarred all over with the marks of savage fights, but he was always   72   _____

ready for just one more fight. He would put his head on one side,   86   _____

as though he were afraid to look his enemy in the face; then he   100   _____

would shoot it out like lightning, and when the big teeth were   112   _____

firmly fixed on the other seal's neck, the other seal might get away   125   _____

if he could, but Sea Catch would not help him.   135   _____

     Yet Sea Catch never chased a beaten seal. That was against the   147   _____

Rules of the Beach. He only wanted room by the sea for a nursery   161   _____

for his offspring; but as there were forty or fifty thousand other   173   _____

seals hunting for the same thing each spring, the whistling,   183   _____

bellowing, roaring, and blowing on the beach were something   192   _____

quite frightful.   194   _____

Needs Work   1   2   3   4   5   Excellent
Paid attention to punctuation

Needs Work   1   2   3   4   5   Excellent
Sounded good

Total Words Read   _____

Total Errors − _____

Correct WPM   _____

from *The Jungle Books*
by Rudyard Kipling

	Words Read	Miscues
Sea Catch was fifteen years old, a huge gray fur seal with almost	13	_____
a mane on his shoulders, and long, wicked dogteeth. When he	24	_____
heaved himself up on his front flippers he stood more than four	36	_____
feet clear of the ground. His weight, if anyone had been bold	48	_____
enough to weigh him, was nearly seven hundred pounds. He was	59	_____
scarred all over with the marks of savage fights, but he was always	72	_____
ready for just one more fight. He would put his head on one side,	86	_____
as though he were afraid to look his enemy in the face; then he	100	_____
would shoot it out like lightning, and when the big teeth were	112	_____
firmly fixed on the other seal's neck, the other seal might get away	125	_____
if he could, but Sea Catch would not help him.	135	_____
Yet Sea Catch never chased a beaten seal. That was against the	147	_____
Rules of the Beach. He only wanted room by the sea for a nursery	161	_____
for his offspring; but as there were forty or fifty thousand other	173	_____
seals hunting for the same thing each spring, the whistling,	183	_____
bellowing, roaring, and blowing on the beach were something	192	_____
quite frightful.	194	_____

Needs Work   1 2 3 4 5   Excellent
Paid attention to punctuation

Needs Work   1 2 3 4 5   Excellent
Sounded good

Total Words Read _____

Total Errors − _____

Correct WPM _____

37

Fiction

from *A Christmas Carol*

by Charles Dickens

	Words Read	Miscues
"Humbug!" said Scrooge; and walked across the room.	8	_____
After several turns, he sat down again. As he threw his head	20	_____
back in the chair, his glance happened to rest upon a bell, a	33	_____
disused bell, that hung in the room, and communicated for some	44	_____
purpose now forgotten with a chamber in the highest story of the	56	_____
building. It was with great astonishment, and with a strange,	66	_____
inexplicable dread, that as he looked, he saw this bell begin to	78	_____
swing. It swung so softly in the outset that it scarcely made a	91	_____
sound; but soon it rang out loudly, and so did every bell in	104	_____
the house.	106	_____
This might have lasted half a minute, or a minute, but it seemed	119	_____
an hour. The bells ceased as they had begun, together. They were	131	_____
succeeded by a clanking noise, deep down below; as if some	142	_____
person were dragging a heavy chain over the casks in the wine-	154	_____
merchant's cellar. Scrooge then remembered to have heard that	162	_____
ghosts in haunted houses were described as dragging chains.	171	_____
The cellar-door flew open with a booming sound, and then he	182	_____
heard the noise much louder, on the floors below; then coming	193	_____
up the stairs; then coming straight towards his door.	202	_____
"It's humbug still!" said Scrooge. "I won't believe it."	211	_____

Needs Work 1 2 3 4 5 Excellent
Paid attention to punctuation

Needs Work 1 2 3 4 5 Excellent
Sounded good

Total Words Read _____

Total Errors − _____

Correct WPM _____

from *A Christmas Carol*
by Charles Dickens

"Humbug!" said Scrooge; and walked across the room.	8 _____
After several turns, he sat down again. As he threw his head	20 _____
back in the chair, his glance happened to rest upon a bell, a	33 _____
disused bell, that hung in the room, and communicated for some	44 _____
purpose now forgotten with a chamber in the highest story of the	56 _____
building. It was with great astonishment, and with a strange,	66 _____
inexplicable dread, that as he looked, he saw this bell begin to	78 _____
swing. It swung so softly in the outset that it scarcely made a	91 _____
sound; but soon it rang out loudly, and so did every bell in	104 _____
the house.	106 _____
This might have lasted half a minute, or a minute, but it seemed	119 _____
an hour. The bells ceased as they had begun, together. They were	131 _____
succeeded by a clanking noise, deep down below; as if some	142 _____
person were dragging a heavy chain over the casks in the wine-	154 _____
merchant's cellar. Scrooge then remembered to have heard that	162 _____
ghosts in haunted houses were described as dragging chains.	171 _____
The cellar-door flew open with a booming sound, and then he	182 _____
heard the noise much louder, on the floors below; then coming	193 _____
up the stairs; then coming straight towards his door.	202 _____
"It's humbug still!" said Scrooge. "I won't believe it."	211 _____

Needs Work   1   2   3   4   5   Excellent
Paid attention to punctuation

Needs Work   1   2   3   4   5   Excellent
Sounded good

Total Words Read _____

Total Errors − _____

Correct WPM _____

38

Nonfiction

from "I See the Promised Land"
by Martin Luther King Jr.

First Reading

	Words Read	Miscues

The issue is the refusal of Memphis to be fair and honest in its | 14 | _____

dealings with its public servants, who happen to be sanitation | 24 | _____

workers. Now, we've got to keep attention on that. That's always | 35 | _____

the problem with a little violence. You know what happened the | 46 | _____

other day, and the press dealt only with the window-breaking. I | 57 | _____

read the articles. They very seldom got around to mentioning the | 68 | _____

fact that one thousand, three hundred sanitation workers were | 77 | _____

on strike, and that Memphis is not being fair to them, and that | 90 | _____

Mayor Loeb is in dire need of a doctor. They didn't get around | 103 | _____

to that. | 105 | _____

Now we're going to march again, and we've got to march | 116 | _____

again, in order to put the issue where it is supposed to be. And | 130 | _____

force everybody to see that there are thirteen hundred of God's | 141 | _____

children here suffering, sometimes going hungry, going through | 149 | _____

dark and dreary nights wondering how this thing is going to come | 161 | _____

out. That's the issue. And we've got to say to the nation: we know | 175 | _____

it's coming out. For when people get caught up with that which is | 188 | _____

right and they are willing to sacrifice for it, there is no stopping | 201 | _____

point short of victory. | 205 | _____

Needs Work   1 2 3 4 5   Excellent
Paid attention to punctuation

Needs Work   1 2 3 4 5   Excellent
Sounded good

Total Words Read _____

Total Errors − _____

Correct WPM _____

from **"I See the Promised Land"**
by Martin Luther King Jr.

	Words Read	Miscues

The issue is the refusal of Memphis to be fair and honest in its | 14 | _____

dealings with its public servants, who happen to be sanitation | 24 | _____

workers. Now, we've got to keep attention on that. That's always | 35 | _____

the problem with a little violence. You know what happened the | 46 | _____

other day, and the press dealt only with the window-breaking. I | 57 | _____

read the articles. They very seldom got around to mentioning the | 68 | _____

fact that one thousand, three hundred sanitation workers were | 77 | _____

on strike, and that Memphis is not being fair to them, and that | 90 | _____

Mayor Loeb is in dire need of a doctor. They didn't get around | 103 | _____

to that. | 105 | _____

   Now we're going to march again, and we've got to march | 116 | _____

again, in order to put the issue where it is supposed to be. And | 130 | _____

force everybody to see that there are thirteen hundred of God's | 141 | _____

children here suffering, sometimes going hungry, going through | 149 | _____

dark and dreary nights wondering how this thing is going to come | 161 | _____

out. That's the issue. And we've got to say to the nation: we know | 175 | _____

it's coming out. For when people get caught up with that which is | 188 | _____

right and they are willing to sacrifice for it, there is no stopping | 201 | _____

point short of victory. | 205 | _____

Needs Work   1 2 3 4 5   Excellent
Paid attention to punctuation

Needs Work   1 2 3 4 5   Excellent
Sounded good

Total Words Read _____

Total Errors − _____

Correct WPM _____

The Great Chicago Fire

39

Nonfiction

First Reading

	Words Read	Miscues

It was 1871 and Chicago was in the midst of a long dry spell.   14 _____
Though it was October, the air was warm and close, and little rain   27 _____
had fallen in weeks. On the night of October 8, many people were   40 _____
sitting outside their homes, trying to cool off in the gusty wind.   52 _____

Daniel "Peg Leg" Sullivan stopped for visits at the homes of his   64 _____
neighbors, including Patrick and Catherine O'Leary. The O'Leary   72 _____
family lived on DeKoven Street on the city's southwest side.   82 _____
Behind their small wooden house was a barn where Mrs. O'Leary   93 _____
kept her dairy cows.   97 _____

The O'Learys had already "turned in" for the evening, and so   108 _____
Sullivan sat down in front of another neighbor's house. Before   118 _____
long, he noticed flames coming from the O'Learys' barn, and he   129 _____
raised the alarm, yelling "Fire!"   134 _____

The O'Leary family was awakened and escaped, but the fire   144 _____
spread quickly. Its sparks flew in the dry wind from rooftop to   156 _____
rooftop. Soon a red glow lit the night sky.   165 _____

The fire burned through the heart of the city and then jumped   177 _____
the river and continued its march north. It raged for over thirty   189 _____
hours, until rain began to fall.   195 _____

When the fire finally died out, much of Chicago was in   206 _____
ruins. However, the O'Leary home still stood, almost untouched   215 _____
by the fire.   218 _____

Needs Work   1   2   3   4   5   Excellent
Paid attention to punctuation

Needs Work   1   2   3   4   5   Excellent
Sounded good

Total Words Read _____

Total Errors − _____

Correct WPM _____

The Great Chicago Fire

	Words Read	Miscues

〜〜〜

It was 1871 and Chicago was in the midst of a long dry spell. | 14 | _____

Though it was October, the air was warm and close, and little rain | 27 | _____

had fallen in weeks. On the night of October 8, many people were | 40 | _____

sitting outside their homes, trying to cool off in the gusty wind. | 52 | _____

Daniel "Peg Leg" Sullivan stopped for visits at the homes of his | 64 | _____

neighbors, including Patrick and Catherine O'Leary. The O'Leary | 72 | _____

family lived on DeKoven Street on the city's southwest side. | 82 | _____

Behind their small wooden house was a barn where Mrs. O'Leary | 93 | _____

kept her dairy cows. | 97 | _____

The O'Learys had already "turned in" for the evening, and so | 108 | _____

Sullivan sat down in front of another neighbor's house. Before | 118 | _____

long, he noticed flames coming from the O'Learys' barn, and he | 129 | _____

raised the alarm, yelling "Fire!" | 134 | _____

The O'Leary family was awakened and escaped, but the fire | 144 | _____

spread quickly. Its sparks flew in the dry wind from rooftop to | 156 | _____

rooftop. Soon a red glow lit the night sky. | 165 | _____

The fire burned through the heart of the city and then jumped | 177 | _____

the river and continued its march north. It raged for over thirty | 189 | _____

hours, until rain began to fall. | 195 | _____

When the fire finally died out, much of Chicago was in | 206 | _____

ruins. However, the O'Leary home still stood, almost untouched | 215 | _____

by the fire. | 218 | _____

Needs Work   1   2   3   4   5   Excellent
Paid attention to punctuation

Needs Work   1   2   3   4   5   Excellent
Sounded good

Total Words Read _____

Total Errors − _____

Correct WPM _____

40
Fiction

Tim's Test

	Words Read	Miscues

As a first-year lifeguard, Tim felt he had to prove himself to | 12 | _____
the other lifeguards. Even though he had the same lifesaving | 22 | _____
certification as everyone else, he wanted to improve his swimming | 32 | _____
and rescue skills. | 35 | _____

Every morning before the lifeguards' official duties began, Tim | 44 | _____
practiced swimming out beyond the breakers. He began by towing | 54 | _____
one float along with him, as every lifeguard did. Day by day, he | 67 | _____
added another and then another float. The added resistance these | 77 | _____
created caused him to work harder. Day by day, Tim's strength | 88 | _____
increased. | 89 | _____

Lifeguards from all the town beaches competed in an annual | 99 | _____
tournament held in the middle of the summer. Tim was nervous | 110 | _____
about participating but excited at the thought of having a chance | 121 | _____
to prove himself. He entered the one-person lifesaving event. | 130 | _____

At the signal, Tim plunged into the surf. With strong, sure | 141 | _____
strokes, he swam toward the drowning "victim"—another | 149 | _____
lifeguard who was playing the part and waiting for rescue. Tim | 160 | _____
reached his victim, secured him safely, and swam rapidly back to | 171 | _____
shore. As he pulled the victim onto shore, a swift glance showed | 183 | _____
that he was the first competitor to reach land. His teammates | 194 | _____
surrounded him, cheering. Tim had won the race and the respect | 205 | _____
of his fellow lifeguards. | 209 | _____

Needs Work 1 2 3 4 5 Excellent
Paid attention to punctuation

Needs Work 1 2 3 4 5 Excellent
Sounded good

Total Words Read _____

Total Errors − _____

Correct WPM _____

Tim's Test

	Words Read	Miscues

As a first-year lifeguard, Tim felt he had to prove himself to | 12 | _____
the other lifeguards. Even though he had the same lifesaving | 22 | _____
certification as everyone else, he wanted to improve his swimming | 32 | _____
and rescue skills. | 35 | _____

Every morning before the lifeguards' official duties began, Tim | 44 | _____
practiced swimming out beyond the breakers. He began by towing | 54 | _____
one float along with him, as every lifeguard did. Day by day, he | 67 | _____
added another and then another float. The added resistance these | 77 | _____
created caused him to work harder. Day by day, Tim's strength | 88 | _____
increased. | 89 | _____

Lifeguards from all the town beaches competed in an annual | 99 | _____
tournament held in the middle of the summer. Tim was nervous | 110 | _____
about participating but excited at the thought of having a chance | 121 | _____
to prove himself. He entered the one-person lifesaving event. | 130 | _____

At the signal, Tim plunged into the surf. With strong, sure | 141 | _____
strokes, he swam toward the drowning "victim"—another | 149 | _____
lifeguard who was playing the part and waiting for rescue. Tim | 160 | _____
reached his victim, secured him safely, and swam rapidly back to | 171 | _____
shore. As he pulled the victim onto shore, a swift glance showed | 183 | _____
that he was the first competitor to reach land. His teammates | 194 | _____
surrounded him, cheering. Tim had won the race and the respect | 205 | _____
of his fellow lifeguards. | 209 | _____

Needs Work   1   2   3   4   5   Excellent
Paid attention to punctuation

Needs Work   1   2   3   4   5   Excellent
Sounded good

Total Words Read _____

Total Errors − _____

Correct WPM _____

41 A Maker of Mobiles

Nonfiction

	Words Read	Miscues

The American artist Alexander Calder became interested in | 8 | _____

making things when he was a child, and even then he often used | 21 | _____

wire in his constructions. When he went to college, he studied | 32 | _____

engineering rather than art. But he quickly realized that art was | 43 | _____

his real passion. He also loved the circus, and many of his early | 56 | _____

art works were small circus figures made with wire and a pliers. | 68 | _____

In about 1930, Calder turned from realistic wire figures to | 78 | _____

abstract ones. He began constructing objects that had circles, | 87 | _____

squares, and other geometric shapes intersecting each other. To | 96 | _____

get the shapes to move, he used small motors or hand cranks. | 108 | _____

Then he went one step beyond these early mobiles. He got the | 120 | _____

shapes in his constructions to move by themselves. | 128 | _____

A mobile may look simple as it shifts in the wind, but it | 141 | _____

requires careful construction to work properly. Calder used his | 150 | _____

engineering knowledge to create his first mobiles. Often these | 159 | _____

consisted of small pieces of brightly painted metal strung by wire | 170 | _____

to a thicker base wire. Calder learned how to find the precise | 182 | _____

point to connect each wire so that all the pieces would sway in | 195 | _____

harmony. In doing so, he created an art form for people all over | 208 | _____

the world to copy and enjoy. | 214 | _____

Needs Work   1   2   3   4   5   Excellent
Paid attention to punctuation

Needs Work   1   2   3   4   5   Excellent
Sounded good

Total Words Read _____

Total Errors − _____

Correct WPM _____

A Maker of Mobiles

	Words Read	Miscues

The American artist Alexander Calder became interested in   8   _____

making things when he was a child, and even then he often used   21   _____

wire in his constructions. When he went to college, he studied   32   _____

engineering rather than art. But he quickly realized that art was   43   _____

his real passion. He also loved the circus, and many of his early   56   _____

art works were small circus figures made with wire and a pliers.   68   _____

In about 1930, Calder turned from realistic wire figures to   78   _____

abstract ones. He began constructing objects that had circles,   87   _____

squares, and other geometric shapes intersecting each other. To   96   _____

get the shapes to move, he used small motors or hand cranks.   108   _____

Then he went one step beyond these early mobiles. He got the   120   _____

shapes in his constructions to move by themselves.   128   _____

A mobile may look simple as it shifts in the wind, but it   141   _____

requires careful construction to work properly. Calder used his   150   _____

engineering knowledge to create his first mobiles. Often these   159   _____

consisted of small pieces of brightly painted metal strung by wire   170   _____

to a thicker base wire. Calder learned how to find the precise   182   _____

point to connect each wire so that all the pieces would sway in   195   _____

harmony. In doing so, he created an art form for people all over   208   _____

the world to copy and enjoy.   214   _____

Needs Work   1   2   3   4   5   Excellent
Paid attention to punctuation

Needs Work   1   2   3   4   5   Excellent
Sounded good

Total Words Read _____

Total Errors − _____

Correct WPM _____

42

Fiction

from "Sigurd the Volsung"

retold by Donna Rosenberg

First Reading

	Words Read	Miscues

With broad steps, the old man strode up to the great trunk of | 13 | _____
the oak tree and plunged his sword deep into the wood, so that | 26 | _____
only the hilt of the sword was visible. While the family and their | 39 | _____
guests stood in amazed silence, the stranger announced, | 47 | _____
"Whoever draws this sword from this oak will have the sword as | 59 | _____
my gift to him, and will find that he never had a better friend in | 74 | _____
time of need." The old man then turned and left the hall. | 86 | _____
Everyone present realized that the visitor had been Odin, the | 96 | _____
All-Father. | 97 | _____

Immediately, all of the noblemen rushed toward the sword in | 107 | _____
the tree. But it would not budge, no matter how hard they tugged. | 120 | _____
Finally, Sigmund put his hand upon the hilt and withdrew the | 131 | _____
sword as easily as if it lay loosely in the wood. | 142 | _____

Sigmund announced, "I am destined to own this sword, for | 152 | _____
I have withdrawn it from its place in the tree. I will never give | 166 | _____
it up, even if a mighty king offers to pay me all the gold that | 181 | _____
he possesses!" | 183 | _____

In time, Sigmund became the noble king of Hunland. So great | 194 | _____
were his courage and cunning, his skill in warfare, and the | 205 | _____
treasure he had won with his sword that his name was known | 217 | _____
throughout the northern lands. | 221 | _____

Needs Work   1   2   3   4   5   Excellent
Paid attention to punctuation

Needs Work   1   2   3   4   5   Excellent
Sounded good

Total Words Read _____

Total Errors − _____

Correct WPM _____

42 from **"Sigurd the Volsung"**

retold by Donna Rosenberg

Fiction

	Words Read	Miscues

With broad steps, the old man strode up to the great trunk of   13 _____
the oak tree and plunged his sword deep into the wood, so that   26 _____
only the hilt of the sword was visible. While the family and their   39 _____
guests stood in amazed silence, the stranger announced,   47 _____
"Whoever draws this sword from this oak will have the sword as   59 _____
my gift to him, and will find that he never had a better friend in   74 _____
time of need." The old man then turned and left the hall.   86 _____
Everyone present realized that the visitor had been Odin, the   96 _____
All-Father.   97 _____

Immediately, all of the noblemen rushed toward the sword in   107 _____
the tree. But it would not budge, no matter how hard they tugged.   120 _____
Finally, Sigmund put his hand upon the hilt and withdrew the   131 _____
sword as easily as if it lay loosely in the wood.   142 _____

Sigmund announced, "I am destined to own this sword, for   152 _____
I have withdrawn it from its place in the tree. I will never give   166 _____
it up, even if a mighty king offers to pay me all the gold that   181 _____
he possesses!"   183 _____

In time, Sigmund became the noble king of Hunland. So great   194 _____
were his courage and cunning, his skill in warfare, and the   205 _____
treasure he had won with his sword that his name was known   217 _____
throughout the northern lands.   221 _____

Needs Work   1   2   3   4   5   Excellent
Paid attention to punctuation

Needs Work   1   2   3   4   5   Excellent
Sounded good

Total Words Read _____

Total Errors − _____

Correct WPM _____

43 Not Just "a White Man's War"

Nonfiction

First Reading

	Words Read	Miscues

President Abraham Lincoln's first call for volunteers to fight in | 10
the Civil War was for whites only. The Civil War was "a white | 23
man's war," northern whites insisted. Its purpose was to preserve | 33
the Union. It was not being fought to end slavery. But by | 45
September of 1862, the sentiment toward black volunteers had | 54
changed. Lincoln had hoped that the war would be short, but it | 66
had already lasted nearly a year and a half. Union enlistments | 77
had fallen off. | 80

In 1863 Lincoln issued the *Emancipation Proclamation.* | 87
It stated that as of January 1, 1863, all slaves residing in the | 100
rebellious Southern states would be forever free. Now, starting | 109
immediately, Union armies could accept black volunteers. | 116

The Southern Rebels' response to Lincoln's call for black troops | 126
was a deadly one. Captives of any Union regiment with black | 137
troops were to be put to death immediately. | 145

African American troops throughout the war distinguished | 152
themselves in battle. By the war's end 186,000 black troops had | 163
participated. They made up nearly 10 percent of Union forces. | 173
These black soldiers saw action in more than 250 battles. Black | 184
soldiers also gave their lives. By the war's end about 38,000 black | 196
troops had died. They died from disease, in battle, and after | 207
capture by Rebel troops. | 211

Needs Work   1   2   3   4   5   Excellent
Paid attention to punctuation

Needs Work   1   2   3   4   5   Excellent
Sounded good

Total Words Read _____

Total Errors − _____

Correct WPM _____

Not Just "a White Man's War"

	Words Read	Miscues

President Abraham Lincoln's first call for volunteers to fight in | 10 | _____
the Civil War was for whites only. The Civil War was "a white | 23 | _____
man's war," northern whites insisted. Its purpose was to preserve | 33 | _____
the Union. It was not being fought to end slavery. But by | 45 | _____
September of 1862, the sentiment toward black volunteers had | 54 | _____
changed. Lincoln had hoped that the war would be short, but it | 66 | _____
had already lasted nearly a year and a half. Union enlistments | 77 | _____
had fallen off. | 80 | _____

In 1863 Lincoln issued the *Emancipation Proclamation.* | 87 | _____
It stated that as of January 1, 1863, all slaves residing in the | 100 | _____
rebellious Southern states would be forever free. Now, starting | 109 | _____
immediately, Union armies could accept black volunteers. | 116 | _____

The Southern Rebels' response to Lincoln's call for black troops | 126 | _____
was a deadly one. Captives of any Union regiment with black | 137 | _____
troops were to be put to death immediately. | 145 | _____

African American troops throughout the war distinguished | 152 | _____
themselves in battle. By the war's end 186,000 black troops had | 163 | _____
participated. They made up nearly 10 percent of Union forces. | 173 | _____
These black soldiers saw action in more than 250 battles. Black | 184 | _____
soldiers also gave their lives. By the war's end about 38,000 black | 196 | _____
troops had died. They died from disease, in battle, and after | 207 | _____
capture by Rebel troops. | 211 | _____

Needs Work 1 2 3 4 5 Excellent
Paid attention to punctuation

Needs Work 1 2 3 4 5 Excellent
Sounded good

Total Words Read _____

Total Errors − _____

Correct WPM _____

44

Fiction

from *The Hound of the Baskervilles*
by Arthur Conan Doyle

First Reading

	Words Read	Miscues

	Words Read	Miscues

That night Sir Charles Baskerville went out as usual for his — 11 _____

nocturnal walk, in the course of which he was in the habit of — 24 _____

smoking a cigar. He never returned. At twelve o'clock Barrymore, — 34 _____

finding the hall door still open, became alarmed. Lighting a — 44 _____

lantern, he went in search of his master. The day had been wet, — 57 _____

and Sir Charles's footmarks were easily traced down the alley. — 67 _____

Halfway down this walk there is a gate which leads out on to the — 81 _____

moor. There were indications that Sir Charles had stood for some — 92 _____

little time here. He then proceeded down the alley, and it was at — 105 _____

the far end of it that his body was discovered. One fact which has — 119 _____

not been explained is the statement of Barrymore that his — 129 _____

master's footprints altered their character from the time that he — 139 _____

passed the moor gate, and that he appeared from thence onward — 150 _____

to have been walking upon his toes. One Murphy, a gypsy horse — 162 _____

dealer, was on the moor at no great distance at the time. He — 175 _____

declares that he heard cries but is unable to state from what — 187 _____

direction they came. No signs of violence were to be discovered — 198 _____

upon Sir Charles's person. — 202 _____

Needs Work   1   2   3   4   5   Excellent
Paid attention to punctuation

Needs Work   1   2   3   4   5   Excellent
Sounded good

Total Words Read _____

Total Errors − _____

Correct WPM _____

from *The Hound of the Baskervilles*

by Arthur Conan Doyle

	Words Read	Miscues

That night Sir Charles Baskerville went out as usual for his — 11

nocturnal walk, in the course of which he was in the habit of — 24

smoking a cigar. He never returned. At twelve o'clock Barrymore, — 34

finding the hall door still open, became alarmed. Lighting a — 44

lantern, he went in search of his master. The day had been wet, — 57

and Sir Charles's footmarks were easily traced down the alley. — 67

Halfway down this walk there is a gate which leads out on to the — 81

moor. There were indications that Sir Charles had stood for some — 92

little time here. He then proceeded down the alley, and it was at — 105

the far end of it that his body was discovered. One fact which has — 119

not been explained is the statement of Barrymore that his — 129

master's footprints altered their character from the time that he — 139

passed the moor gate, and that he appeared from thence onward — 150

to have been walking upon his toes. One Murphy, a gypsy horse — 162

dealer, was on the moor at no great distance at the time. He — 175

declares that he heard cries but is unable to state from what — 187

direction they came. No signs of violence were to be discovered — 198

upon Sir Charles's person. — 202

Needs Work   1   2   3   4   5   Excellent
Paid attention to punctuation

Needs Work   1   2   3   4   5   Excellent
Sounded good

Total Words Read _____

Total Errors − _____

Correct WPM _____

45

Fiction

from **"Hollywood and the Pits"**

by Cherylene Lee

First Reading

	Words Read	Miscues

In Las Vegas our sister act was part of a show called "Oriental   13   _____

Holiday." The show was about a Hollywood producer going to the   24   _____

Far East, finding undiscovered talent, and bringing it back to the   35   _____

U.S. We did two shows a night in the main showroom, one at   48   _____

eight and one at twelve, and on weekends a third show at two in   62   _____

the morning. It ran the entire summer often to standing-room-   72   _____

only audiences—a thousand people a show.   78   _____

Our sister act worked because of the age and height difference.   89   _____

My sister then was fourteen and nearly five foot two; I was seven   102   _____

and very small for my age—people thought we were cute. We had   115   _____

song-and-dance routines to old tunes like "Ma, He's Making Eyes   125   _____

at Me," "Together," and "I'm Following You," and my father hired a   137   _____

writer to adapt the lyrics to "I Enjoy Being a Girl," which came   150   _____

out "We Enjoy Being Chinese." We also told corny jokes, but the   162   _____

Las Vegas audience seemed to enjoy it. Here we were, two kids,   174   _____

staying up late and jumping around, and getting paid besides. To   185   _____

me the applause sometimes sounded like static, sometimes like   194   _____

distant waves. It always amazed me when people applauded.   203   _____

Needs Work   1 2 3 4 5   Excellent

Paid attention to punctuation

Needs Work   1 2 3 4 5   Excellent

Sounded good

Total Words Read _____

Total Errors – _____

Correct WPM _____

45

Fiction

from **"Hollywood and the Pits"**
by Cherylene Lee

	Words Read	Miscues

In Las Vegas our sister act was part of a show called "Oriental   13 _____
Holiday." The show was about a Hollywood producer going to the   24 _____
Far East, finding undiscovered talent, and bringing it back to the   35 _____
U.S. We did two shows a night in the main showroom, one at   48 _____
eight and one at twelve, and on weekends a third show at two in   62 _____
the morning. It ran the entire summer often to standing-room-   72 _____
only audiences—a thousand people a show.   78 _____

Our sister act worked because of the age and height difference.   89 _____
My sister then was fourteen and nearly five foot two; I was seven   102 _____
and very small for my age—people thought we were cute. We had   115 _____
song-and-dance routines to old tunes like "Ma, He's Making Eyes   125 _____
at Me," "Together," and "I'm Following You," and my father hired a   137 _____
writer to adapt the lyrics to "I Enjoy Being a Girl," which came   150 _____
out "We Enjoy Being Chinese." We also told corny jokes, but the   162 _____
Las Vegas audience seemed to enjoy it. Here we were, two kids,   174 _____
staying up late and jumping around, and getting paid besides. To   185 _____
me the applause sometimes sounded like static, sometimes like   194 _____
distant waves. It always amazed me when people applauded.   203 _____

Needs Work   1   2   3   4   5   Excellent
Paid attention to punctuation

Needs Work   1   2   3   4   5   Excellent
Sounded good

Total Words Read   _____

Total Errors   − _____

Correct WPM   _____

46

Fiction

from **"Miss Muriel"**
by Ann Petry

	Words Read	Miscues

When I listen to Dottle [tell stories,] I can see the old black · 13 · _____
preacher who spent the night in a haunted house. I see him · 25 · _____
approaching the house, the wind blowing his coattails, and finally · 35 · _____
him taking refuge inside because of the violence of the storm. He · 47 · _____
lights a fire in the fireplace and sits down by it and rubs his · 61 · _____
hands together, warming them. As he sits there, he hears heavy · 72 · _____
footsteps coming down the stairs (and Dottle makes his hand go · 83 · _____
thump, thump, thump on the bank of the creek) and the biggest · 95 · _____
cat the old man has ever seen comes in and sits down, looks at · 109 · _____
the old preacher, looks around, and says, "Has Martin got here · 120 · _____
yet?" The old man is too startled and too nervous to answer. · 132 · _____
He hears heavy footsteps again—thump, thump, thump. And · 141 · _____
a second cat, much bigger than the first one, comes in, and sits · 154 · _____
down right next to the old preacher. Both cats stare at him, and · 167 · _____
then the second cat says to the first cat, "Has Martin got here · 180 · _____
yet?" and the first cat shakes his head. There is something so · 192 · _____
speculative in their glance that the old man gets more and · 203 · _____
more uneasy. He wonders if they are deciding to eat him. · 214 · _____

Needs Work   1 2 3 4 5   Excellent
Paid attention to punctuation

Needs Work   1 2 3 4 5   Excellent
Sounded good

Total Words Read _____

Total Errors − _____

Correct WPM _____

from "Miss Muriel"

by Ann Petry

	Words Read	Miscues
When I listen to Dottle [tell stories,] I can see the old black	13	_____
preacher who spent the night in a haunted house. I see him	25	_____
approaching the house, the wind blowing his coattails, and finally	35	_____
him taking refuge inside because of the violence of the storm. He	47	_____
lights a fire in the fireplace and sits down by it and rubs his	61	_____
hands together, warming them. As he sits there, he hears heavy	72	_____
footsteps coming down the stairs (and Dottle makes his hand go	83	_____
thump, thump, thump on the bank of the creek) and the biggest	95	_____
cat the old man has ever seen comes in and sits down, looks at	109	_____
the old preacher, looks around, and says, "Has Martin got here	120	_____
yet?" The old man is too startled and too nervous to answer.	132	_____
He hears heavy footsteps again—thump, thump, thump. And	141	_____
a second cat, much bigger than the first one, comes in, and sits	154	_____
down right next to the old preacher. Both cats stare at him, and	167	_____
then the second cat says to the first cat, "Has Martin got here	180	_____
yet?" and the first cat shakes his head. There is something so	192	_____
speculative in their glance that the old man gets more and	203	_____
more uneasy. He wonders if they are deciding to eat him.	214	_____

Needs Work   1   2   3   4   5   Excellent
Paid attention to punctuation

Needs Work   1   2   3   4   5   Excellent
Sounded good

Total Words Read   _____

Total Errors   − _____

Correct WPM   _____

47
Nonfiction

The Story of the U.S. Census

First Reading

	Words Read	Miscues

The first national census in the United States was taken in | 11 | _____

1790. Seventeen U.S. marshals and 200 assistants rode on | 20 | _____

horseback all over the country to count the population. They | 30 | _____

recorded information on scraps of paper. It took 18 months to | 41 | _____

count 3.9 million people—not including enslaved persons. | 49 | _____

Technology became a part of the census starting in 1890. | 59 | _____

Census takers punched holes in cards to record answers to their | 70 | _____

questions. The cards were fed into a special electrical machine | 80 | _____

that added up the number of holes. | 87 | _____

By 1900 the country—and the census—had really grown. | 97 | _____

Approximately 53,000 census takers went door-to-door asking | 104 | _____

22 questions, including name, age, sex, race, and birthplace. | 113 | _____

For the 1950 census, the Census Bureau decided to take | 123 | _____

advantage of new advances in technology. It used a computer, | 133 | _____

called UNIVAC, that filled an entire room. By 1960 the | 143 | _____

population was too big for census takers to question people | 153 | _____

individually. The Census Bureau began to mail many of the forms. | 164 | _____

The most recent census took place in 2000. Ninety-eight | 173 | _____

million census forms were mailed. Census takers personally | 181 | _____

delivered about 22 million forms. | 186 | _____

Two kinds of forms were mailed out. The short form asked | 197 | _____

only seven questions. Five out of six homes received the short | 208 | _____

forms. The long form had 52 questions! | 215 | _____

Needs Work   1 2 3 4 5   Excellent
Paid attention to punctuation

Needs Work   1 2 3 4 5   Excellent
Sounded good

Total Words Read   _____

Total Errors − _____

Correct WPM   _____

The Story of the U.S. Census

	Words Read	Miscues
The first national census in the United States was taken in	11	_____
1790. Seventeen U.S. marshals and 200 assistants rode on	20	_____
horseback all over the country to count the population. They	30	_____
recorded information on scraps of paper. It took 18 months to	41	_____
count 3.9 million people—not including enslaved persons.	49	_____
Technology became a part of the census starting in 1890.	59	_____
Census takers punched holes in cards to record answers to their	70	_____
questions. The cards were fed into a special electrical machine	80	_____
that added up the number of holes.	87	_____
By 1900 the country—and the census—had really grown.	97	_____
Approximately 53,000 census takers went door-to-door asking	104	_____
22 questions, including name, age, sex, race, and birthplace.	113	_____
For the 1950 census, the Census Bureau decided to take	123	_____
advantage of new advances in technology. It used a computer,	133	_____
called UNIVAC, that filled an entire room. By 1960 the	143	_____
population was too big for census takers to question people	153	_____
individually. The Census Bureau began to mail many of the forms.	164	_____
The most recent census took place in 2000. Ninety-eight	173	_____
million census forms were mailed. Census takers personally	181	_____
delivered about 22 million forms.	186	_____
Two kinds of forms were mailed out. The short form asked	197	_____
only seven questions. Five out of six homes received the short	208	_____
forms. The long form had 52 questions!	215	_____

Needs Work 1 2 3 4 5 Excellent
Paid attention to punctuation

Needs Work 1 2 3 4 5 Excellent
Sounded good

Total Words Read _____

Total Errors − _____

Correct WPM _____

48
Fiction

from *The Aeneid*
by **Homer**
retold by Donna Rosenberg

	Words Read	Miscues

As the Trojans watched, clouds suddenly turned day into night. | 10 | _____

The men cried out with dread as flashes of lightning illuminated | 21 | _____

the clouds and the rumbling of thunder surrounded them. Aeneas | 31 | _____

stretched his arms toward the heavens and cried, "Compared to us, | 42 | _____

three and four times blessed are those who were fated to die | 54 | _____

before their fathers' eyes upon the plain of Troy!" | 63 | _____

His words were followed by a shrieking gust of wind that struck | 75 | _____

his sail full force and raised mountainous waves, causing the oars | 86 | _____

to snap and the ship to turn broadside to the waves. As water | 99 | _____

cascaded into the ship, the sailors were washed overboard. Some | 109 | _____

were carried high upon the crests, while others could glimpse the | 120 | _____

ground between the swells. The storm drove three ships upon | 130 | _____

concealed rocks; three others were forced upon a willow sandbar. | 140 | _____

One was completely swallowed by a swirling whirlpool of waters. | 150 | _____

The sea now wore the planking of ships and the bodies of men | 163 | _____

intermingled with its collection of weapons of war and Trojan | 173 | _____

treasure. | 174 | _____

When Neptune became aware of this wild turbulence, he | 183 | _____

raised his head above the waves in order to learn more about the | 196 | _____

storm. He immediately recognized his sister Juno's anger behind | 205 | _____

the destruction of Aeneas's fleet. | 210 | _____

Needs Work   1   2   3   4   5   Excellent
Paid attention to punctuation

Needs Work   1   2   3   4   5   Excellent
Sounded good

Total Words Read _____

Total Errors − _____

Correct WPM _____

48

Fiction

from *The Aeneid*

by Homer

retold by Donna Rosenberg

	Words Read	Miscues

As the Trojans watched, clouds suddenly turned day into night. The men cried out with dread as flashes of lightning illuminated the clouds and the rumbling of thunder surrounded them. Aeneas stretched his arms toward the heavens and cried, "Compared to us, three and four times blessed are those who were fated to die before their fathers' eyes upon the plain of Troy!"

His words were followed by a shrieking gust of wind that struck his sail full force and raised mountainous waves, causing the oars to snap and the ship to turn broadside to the waves. As water cascaded into the ship, the sailors were washed overboard. Some were carried high upon the crests, while others could glimpse the ground between the swells. The storm drove three ships upon concealed rocks; three others were forced upon a willow sandbar. One was completely swallowed by a swirling whirlpool of waters. The sea now wore the planking of ships and the bodies of men intermingled with its collection of weapons of war and Trojan treasure.

When Neptune became aware of this wild turbulence, he raised his head above the waves in order to learn more about the storm. He immediately recognized his sister Juno's anger behind the destruction of Aeneas's fleet.

Words Read
10
21
31
42
54
63
75
86
99
109
120
130
140
150
163
173
174
183
196
205
210

Needs Work   1   2   3   4   5   Excellent
Paid attention to punctuation

Needs Work   1   2   3   4   5   Excellent
Sounded good

Total Words Read _____

Total Errors − _____

Correct WPM _____

49

Nonfiction

from *The Thread That Runs So True*
by Jesse Stuart

First Reading

	Words Read	Miscues

When I walked down the broad center aisle and pulled on the — 12 ____

bell rope, the soft tones sounded over the tobacco, corn, and cane — 24 ____

fields and the lush green valley; with the ringing of this bell, my — 37 ____

school had begun. I knew that not half the pupils in the school — 50 ____

census were here. There were 104 in the school census, of school — 62 ____

age, for whom the state sent per capita money to pay for their — 75 ____

schooling. I had thirty-five pupils. I thought the soft tones of this — 87 ____

school bell through the rising mists and over warm cultivated — 97 ____

fields where parents and their children were trying to eke out a — 109 ____

bare subsistence from the soil might bring back warm memories — 119 ____

of happy school days. For I remembered the tones of the Plum — 131 ____

Grove school bell, and how I had longed to be back in school — 144 ____

after I had quit at the age of nine to work for twenty-five cents a — 159 ____

day to help support my family. If I could have, I would have — 172 ____

returned to school when I heard the Plum Grove bell. So I rang — 185 ____

the bell and called the Lonesome Valley pupils back to school— — 196 ____

back to books and play. — 201 ____

Needs Work   1   2   3   4   5   Excellent
Paid attention to punctuation

Needs Work   1   2   3   4   5   Excellent
Sounded good

Total Words Read _____

Total Errors − _____

Correct WPM _____

from *The Thread That Runs So True*
by Jesse Stuart

When I walked down the broad center aisle and pulled on the	12	_____
bell rope, the soft tones sounded over the tobacco, corn, and cane	24	_____
fields and the lush green valley; with the ringing of this bell, my	37	_____
school had begun. I knew that not half the pupils in the school	50	_____
census were here. There were 104 in the school census, of school	62	_____
age, for whom the state sent per capita money to pay for their	75	_____
schooling. I had thirty-five pupils. I thought the soft tones of this	87	_____
school bell through the rising mists and over warm cultivated	97	_____
fields where parents and their children were trying to eke out a	109	_____
bare subsistence from the soil might bring back warm memories	119	_____
of happy school days. For I remembered the tones of the Plum	131	_____
Grove school bell, and how I had longed to be back in school	144	_____
after I had quit at the age of nine to work for twenty-five cents a	159	_____
day to help support my family. If I could have, I would have	172	_____
returned to school when I heard the Plum Grove bell. So I rang	185	_____
the bell and called the Lonesome Valley pupils back to school—	196	_____
back to books and play.	201	_____

Needs Work   1   2   3   4   5   Excellent
Paid attention to punctuation

Needs Work   1   2   3   4   5   Excellent
Sounded good

Total Words Read _____

Total Errors − _____

Correct WPM _____

50

Fiction

from "Country Girl"

by Luis Tablanca
translated by Alida Malkus

	Words Read	Miscues

Many poor people flock out from the villages, looking for a few | 12 | _____

days' work, eager to eat until they are full once more, and to pass | 26 | _____

a merry time in the coffee plantations. Neither cooks nor servants | 37 | _____

remain in the houses; in the streets there are no porters, nor any | 50 | _____

of the barefooted ne'er-do-wells who lounge about in the sun in | 61 | _____

every village plaza. All of them set out on a great excursion to hire | 75 | _____

out as day laborers at the haciendas. Young and old, men and | 87 | _____

women, find jobs with good pay in these days. They all know | 99 | _____

the work. The coffee branches are heavy and drooping, and must | 110 | _____

be relieved of their burden before the berries fall and are lost. | 122 | _____

Whoever presents himself is hired at once, without question as | 132 | _____

to who he is or where he comes from. And thus for some weeks | 146 | _____

the most widely assorted and strange people from the poor of | 157 | _____

country and village are gathered together. | 163 | _____

Old Juan Cuevas had a coffee plantation. He had planted it in | 175 | _____

his youth with his own hands. It was not very large, nor very | 188 | _____

good; but when the crop began to ripen, he had to hire at least | 202 | _____

twenty laborers to gather it in. | 208 | _____

Needs Work   1   2   3   4   5   Excellent
Paid attention to punctuation

Needs Work   1   2   3   4   5   Excellent
Sounded good

Total Words Read _____

Total Errors − _____

Correct WPM _____

50

Fiction

from "Country Girl"

by Luis Tablanca
translated by Alida Malkus

	Words Read	Miscues

Many poor people flock out from the villages, looking for a few — 12 _____

days' work, eager to eat until they are full once more, and to pass — 26 _____

a merry time in the coffee plantations. Neither cooks nor servants — 37 _____

remain in the houses; in the streets there are no porters, nor any — 50 _____

of the barefooted ne'er-do-wells who lounge about in the sun in — 61 _____

every village plaza. All of them set out on a great excursion to hire — 75 _____

out as day laborers at the haciendas. Young and old, men and — 87 _____

women, find jobs with good pay in these days. They all know — 99 _____

the work. The coffee branches are heavy and drooping, and must — 110 _____

be relieved of their burden before the berries fall and are lost. — 122 _____

Whoever presents himself is hired at once, without question as — 132 _____

to who he is or where he comes from. And thus for some weeks — 146 _____

the most widely assorted and strange people from the poor of — 157 _____

country and village are gathered together. — 163 _____

Old Juan Cuevas had a coffee plantation. He had planted it in — 175 _____

his youth with his own hands. It was not very large, nor very — 188 _____

good; but when the crop began to ripen, he had to hire at least — 202 _____

twenty laborers to gather it in. — 208 _____

Needs Work 1 2 3 4 5 Excellent
Paid attention to punctuation

Needs Work 1 2 3 4 5 Excellent
Sounded good

Total Words Read _____

Total Errors − _____

Correct WPM _____

51
Nonfiction

Passing the Buck

First Reading

	Words Read	Miscues

Recently, reports came into the Spokane regional Game
Department office about a deer being kept as a pet. This is illegal.
No facts about this report or names of persons involved could be
found, but after some research the story was found to be true.
When a wildlife agent went to the farm where the fawn was
reportedly being held, he found that the people had moved
away. The young deer was nowhere to be found.

Off and on during the summer, stories circulated about a
young deer that sometimes wandered into houses near Sherman
Pass. The local people were pleased and excited by the young
deer's presence, except when it raided their gardens.

The fawn made it through the fall and winter, showing up
again in the spring. By now the deer was a yearling. It was larger
and seemed to be quite tame. It followed humans around their
homes and did little tricks, such as begging for food and playing
with children.

When this wild creature was taken from its natural environment
by people who tried to tame it, its behavior patterns changed. It no
longer behaved like a wild animal, and in many ways it did not
know how to protect itself or how to survive on its own.

Words Read
8
21
33
45
57
67
76
86
95
106
114
125
139
150
162
164
174
187
200
212

Needs Work   1 2 3 4 5   Excellent
Paid attention to punctuation

Needs Work   1 2 3 4 5   Excellent
Sounded good

Total Words Read _____

Total Errors − _____

Correct WPM _____

Passing the Buck

	Words Read	Miscues
Recently, reports came into the Spokane regional Game	8	_____
Department office about a deer being kept as a pet. This is illegal.	21	_____
No facts about this report or names of persons involved could be	33	_____
found, but after some research the story was found to be true.	45	_____
When a wildlife agent went to the farm where the fawn was	57	_____
reportedly being held, he found that the people had moved	67	_____
away. The young deer was nowhere to be found.	76	_____
Off and on during the summer, stories circulated about a	86	_____
young deer that sometimes wandered into houses near Sherman	95	_____
Pass. The local people were pleased and excited by the young	106	_____
deer's presence, except when it raided their gardens.	114	_____
The fawn made it through the fall and winter, showing up	125	_____
again in the spring. By now the deer was a yearling. It was larger	139	_____
and seemed to be quite tame. It followed humans around their	150	_____
homes and did little tricks, such as begging for food and playing	162	_____
with children.	164	_____
When this wild creature was taken from its natural environment	174	_____
by people who tried to tame it, its behavior patterns changed. It no	187	_____
longer behaved like a wild animal, and in many ways it did not	200	_____
know how to protect itself or how to survive on its own.	212	_____

Needs Work   1   2   3   4   5   Excellent
Paid attention to punctuation

Needs Work   1   2   3   4   5   Excellent
Sounded good

Total Words Read _____

Total Errors − _____

Correct WPM _____

52
Fiction

from *The Witch of Blackbird Pond*
by Elizabeth George Speare

	Words Read	Miscues

It took nine days for the *Dolphin* to make the forty-three mile · 12 · _____

voyage from Saybrook to Wethersfield. As though the ship were · 22 · _____

bewitched, from the moment they left Saybrook everything went · 31 · _____

wrong. With the narrowing of the river the fresh sea breeze · 42 · _____

dropped behind, and by sunset it died away altogether. The sails · 53 · _____

sagged limp and soundless, and the *Dolphin* rolled sickeningly in · 63 · _____

midstream. On one or two evenings a temporary breeze raised · 73 · _____

their hopes and sent the ship ahead a few miles, only to die away · 87 · _____

again. In the morning Kit could scarcely tell that they had moved. · 99 · _____

The dense brown forest on either side never seemed to vary, and · 111 · _____

ahead there was only a new bend in the river to tantalize her. · 124 · _____

"How can you stand it?" she fumed to a redheaded sailor who · 136 · _____

was taking advantage of the windless hours to give the carved · 147 · _____

dolphin at the prow a fresh coat of paint. "Doesn't the wind ever · 160 · _____

blow on this river?" · 164 · _____

"Mighty seldom, ma'am," he responded with indifferent good · 172 · _____

humor. "You get used to it. We'll spend most of the summer · 184 · _____

waiting for a breeze, going or coming." · 191 · _____

Needs Work   1 2 3 4 5   Excellent
Paid attention to punctuation

Needs Work   1 2 3 4 5   Excellent
Sounded good

Total Words Read _____

Total Errors − _____

Correct WPM _____

52
Fiction

from *The Witch of Blackbird Pond*
by Elizabeth George Speare

	Words Read	Miscues

⎯∞∞∞⎯

It took nine days for the *Dolphin* to make the forty-three mile	12	_____
voyage from Saybrook to Wethersfield. As though the ship were	22	_____
bewitched, from the moment they left Saybrook everything went	31	_____
wrong. With the narrowing of the river the fresh sea breeze	42	_____
dropped behind, and by sunset it died away altogether. The sails	53	_____
sagged limp and soundless, and the *Dolphin* rolled sickeningly in	63	_____
midstream. On one or two evenings a temporary breeze raised	73	_____
their hopes and sent the ship ahead a few miles, only to die away	87	_____
again. In the morning Kit could scarcely tell that they had moved.	99	_____
The dense brown forest on either side never seemed to vary, and	111	_____
ahead there was only a new bend in the river to tantalize her.	124	_____
"How can you stand it?" she fumed to a redheaded sailor who	136	_____
was taking advantage of the windless hours to give the carved	147	_____
dolphin at the prow a fresh coat of paint. "Doesn't the wind ever	160	_____
blow on this river?"	164	_____
"Mighty seldom, ma'am," he responded with indifferent good	172	_____
humor. "You get used to it. We'll spend most of the summer	184	_____
waiting for a breeze, going or coming."	191	_____

Needs Work   1   2   3   4   5   Excellent
> *Paid attention to punctuation*

Needs Work   1   2   3   4   5   Excellent
> *Sounded good*

Total Words Read   _____

Total Errors   −_____

Correct WPM   _____

53

Fiction

from *Winter Thunder*

by Mari Sandoz

	Words Read	Miscues

With Chuck, sixteen and almost as tall as a man, beside her, Lecia Terry pushed the frightened huddle of children together and hurried them away downwind into the wall of storm. Once she tried to look back through the smother of snow, wishing that they might have taken the rope and shovel from the toolbox. But there was no time to dig for them on the under side now.

Back at the bus thick smoke was sliding out the door into the snow that swept along the side. Flames began to lick up under the leaning windows, the caking of ice suddenly running from them. The glass held one moment and burst, and the flames whipped out, torn away by the storm as the whole bus was suddenly a wet, shining yellow that blistered and browned with the heat. Then there was a dull explosion above the roar of the wind, and down the slope the fleeing little group heard it and thought they saw a dark fragment fly past overhead.

"Well, I guess that was the gas tank going," Chuck shouted as he tried to peer back under his shielding cap. But there was only the blizzard closed in around them, and the instinctive fear that these swift storms brought to all living creatures, particularly the young.

Words Read
12
22
33
45
57
69
82
95
105
116
130
140
153
166
171
183
196
207
216
218

Needs Work 1 2 3 4 5 Excellent
Paid attention to punctuation

Needs Work 1 2 3 4 5 Excellent
Sounded good

Total Words Read _____

Total Errors − _____

Correct WPM _____

53

Fiction

from *Winter Thunder*
by Mari Sandoz

	Words Read	Miscues

With Chuck, sixteen and almost as tall as a man, beside her, Lecia Terry pushed the frightened huddle of children together and hurried them away downwind into the wall of storm. Once she tried to look back through the smother of snow, wishing that they might have taken the rope and shovel from the toolbox. But there was no time to dig for them on the under side now.

Back at the bus thick smoke was sliding out the door into the snow that swept along the side. Flames began to lick up under the leaning windows, the caking of ice suddenly running from them. The glass held one moment and burst, and the flames whipped out, torn away by the storm as the whole bus was suddenly a wet, shining yellow that blistered and browned with the heat. Then there was a dull explosion above the roar of the wind, and down the slope the fleeing little group heard it and thought they saw a dark fragment fly past overhead.

"Well, I guess that was the gas tank going," Chuck shouted as he tried to peer back under his shielding cap. But there was only the blizzard closed in around them, and the instinctive fear that these swift storms brought to all living creatures, particularly the young.

Words Read
12
22
33
45
57
69
82
95
105
116
130
140
153
166
171
183
196
207
216
218

Needs Work   1   2   3   4   5   Excellent
Paid attention to punctuation

Needs Work   1   2   3   4   5   Excellent
Sounded good

Total Words Read _____

Total Errors − _____

Correct WPM _____

54

Nonfiction

Operation Desert Fire

	Words Read	Miscues

Over the years, Red Adair and his crew put out dozens of | 12 | _____
seemingly unstoppable oil well fires. Then, in 1991, the Persian | 22 | _____
Gulf War resulted in a challenge that made all previous fires seem | 34 | _____
like child's play. Earlier, the nation of Iraq had invaded and | 45 | _____
conquered its tiny oil-rich neighbor, Kuwait. The United States | 54 | _____
and other nations responded by driving the Iraqis out of Kuwait | 65 | _____
in Operation Desert Storm. | 69 | _____

Before leaving Kuwait, however, the Iraqis ignited over 500 oil | 79 | _____
wells. These fires burned more than six million barrels of oil a day. | 92 | _____
Crude oil was going up in flames at a rate of $1,000 a second! | 106 | _____
The black smoke was so dense it blotted out the noonday sun and | 119 | _____
fouled the atmosphere as far away as Hawaii. It seemed as if the | 132 | _____
whole nation was on fire. | 137 | _____

It was little wonder that the task of extinguishing these fires | 148 | _____
was monumental. The job was far too big for the 75-year-old | 159 | _____
Red Adair and his company to do alone, so three other firefighting | 171 | _____
companies joined the effort. Nobody had ever seen a situation | 181 | _____
quite like this one. There was nothing but fire, smoke, and sticky | 193 | _____
pools of oil all over the place. | 200 | _____

Needs Work   1   2   3   4   5   Excellent
    Paid attention to punctuation

Needs Work   1   2   3   4   5   Excellent
    Sounded good

Total Words Read _____

Total Errors − _____

Correct WPM _____

54 Operation Desert Fire

	Words Read	Miscues
Over the years, Red Adair and his crew put out dozens of	12	_____
seemingly unstoppable oil well fires. Then, in 1991, the Persian	22	_____
Gulf War resulted in a challenge that made all previous fires seem	34	_____
like child's play. Earlier, the nation of Iraq had invaded and	45	_____
conquered its tiny oil-rich neighbor, Kuwait. The United States	54	_____
and other nations responded by driving the Iraqis out of Kuwait	65	_____
in Operation Desert Storm.	69	_____
Before leaving Kuwait, however, the Iraqis ignited over 500 oil	79	_____
wells. These fires burned more than six million barrels of oil a day.	92	_____
Crude oil was going up in flames at a rate of $1,000 a second!	106	_____
The black smoke was so dense it blotted out the noonday sun and	119	_____
fouled the atmosphere as far away as Hawaii. It seemed as if the	132	_____
whole nation was on fire.	137	_____
It was little wonder that the task of extinguishing these fires	148	_____
was monumental. The job was far too big for the 75-year-old	159	_____
Red Adair and his company to do alone, so three other firefighting	171	_____
companies joined the effort. Nobody had ever seen a situation	181	_____
quite like this one. There was nothing but fire, smoke, and sticky	193	_____
pools of oil all over the place.	200	_____

Needs Work 1 2 3 4 5 Excellent
Paid attention to punctuation

Needs Work 1 2 3 4 5 Excellent
Sounded good

Total Words Read _____

Total Errors − _____

Correct WPM _____

55

Fiction

from "The Magic Barrel"
by Bernard Malamud

First Reading

	Words Read	Miscues

Leo rushed downstairs, grabbed up the Bronx telephone book, — 9 —

and searched for [matchmaker] Salzman's home address. He was — 18 —

not listed, nor was his office. Neither was he in the Manhattan — 30 —

book. But Leo remembered having written down the address on — 40 —

a slip of paper after he had read Salzman's advertisement in the — 52 —

"personals" column of the *Forward*. He ran up to his room and — 64 —

tore through his papers, without luck. It was exasperating. Just — 74 —

when he needed the matchmaker he was nowhere to be found. — 85 —

Fortunately Leo remembered to look in his wallet. There on a — 96 —

card he found his name written and a Bronx address. No phone — 108 —

number was listed, the reason—Leo now recalled—he had — 118 —

originally communicated with Salzman by letter. He got on his — 128 —

coat, put a hat on over his skullcap and hurried to the subway — 141 —

station. All the way to the far end of the Bronx he sat on the — 156 —

edge of his seat. He was more than once tempted to take out the — 170 —

picture and see if the girl's face was as he remembered it, but he — 184 —

refrained, allowing the snapshot to remain in his inside coat — 194 —

pocket, content to have her so close. — 201 —

Needs Work   1   2   3   4   5   Excellent
_____
Paid attention to punctuation

Needs Work   1   2   3   4   5   Excellent
_____
Sounded good

Total Words Read _____

Total Errors − _____

Correct WPM _____

55 from **"The Magic Barrel"**
by Bernard Malamud

Fiction

	Words Read	Miscues

Leo rushed downstairs, grabbed up the Bronx telephone book, **9**
and searched for [matchmaker] Salzman's home address. He was **18**
not listed, nor was his office. Neither was he in the Manhattan **30**
book. But Leo remembered having written down the address on **40**
a slip of paper after he had read Salzman's advertisement in the **52**
"personals" column of the *Forward*. He ran up to his room and **64**
tore through his papers, without luck. It was exasperating. Just **74**
when he needed the matchmaker he was nowhere to be found. **85**
Fortunately Leo remembered to look in his wallet. There on a **96**
card he found his name written and a Bronx address. No phone **108**
number was listed, the reason—Leo now recalled—he had **118**
originally communicated with Salzman by letter. He got on his **128**
coat, put a hat on over his skullcap and hurried to the subway **141**
station. All the way to the far end of the Bronx he sat on the **156**
edge of his seat. He was more than once tempted to take out the **170**
picture and see if the girl's face was as he remembered it, but he **184**
refrained, allowing the snapshot to remain in his inside coat **194**
pocket, content to have her so close. **201**

Needs Work 1 2 3 4 5 Excellent
Paid attention to punctuation

Needs Work 1 2 3 4 5 Excellent
Sounded good

Total Words Read _____

Total Errors – _____

Correct WPM _____

56
Fiction

from "What Men Live By"
by Leo Tolstoy
translated by Louise and Aylmer Maude

First Reading

	Words Read	Miscues

People said that no one sewed boots so neatly and strongly as   12   _____
Simon's workman, Michael; from all the district round people   21   _____
came to Simon for their boots, and he began to be well off.   34   _____

One winter day, as Simon and Michael sat working, a carriage   45   _____
on sledge-runners, with three horses and with bells, drove up to   56   _____
the hut. They looked out of the window; the carriage stopped at   68   _____
their door, a fine servant jumped down from the box and opened   80   _____
the door. A gentleman in a fur coat got out and walked up to   94   _____
Simon's hut. Up jumped [Simon's wife] Matrëna and opened the   104   _____
door wide. The gentleman stooped to enter the hut, and when he   116   _____
drew himself up again his head nearly reached the ceiling and he   128   _____
seemed quite to fill his end of the room.   137   _____

Simon rose, bowed, and looked at the gentleman with   146   _____
astonishment. He had never seen any one like him. Simon himself   157   _____
was lean, Michael was thin, and Matrëna was dry as a bone, but   170   _____
this man was like someone from another world: red-faced, burly,   180   _____
with a neck like a bull's, and looking altogether as if he were cast   194   _____
in iron.   196   _____

The gentleman puffed, threw off his fur coat, sat down on the   208   _____
bench, and said, "Which of you is the master bootmaker?"   218   _____

Needs Work   1 2 3 4 5   Excellent
Paid attention to punctuation

Needs Work   1 2 3 4 5   Excellent
Sounded good

Total Words Read   _____

Total Errors − _____

Correct WPM   _____

111

56

Fiction

from "What Men Live By"

by Leo Tolstoy

translated by Louise and Aylmer Maude

People said that no one sewed boots so neatly and strongly as	12
Simon's workman, Michael; from all the district round people	21
came to Simon for their boots, and he began to be well off.	34
One winter day, as Simon and Michael sat working, a carriage	45
on sledge-runners, with three horses and with bells, drove up to	56
the hut. They looked out of the window; the carriage stopped at	68
their door, a fine servant jumped down from the box and opened	80
the door. A gentleman in a fur coat got out and walked up to	94
Simon's hut. Up jumped [Simon's wife] Matrëna and opened the	104
door wide. The gentleman stooped to enter the hut, and when he	116
drew himself up again his head nearly reached the ceiling and he	128
seemed quite to fill his end of the room.	137
Simon rose, bowed, and looked at the gentleman with	146
astonishment. He had never seen any one like him. Simon himself	157
was lean, Michael was thin, and Matrëna was dry as a bone, but	170
this man was like someone from another world: red-faced, burly,	180
with a neck like a bull's, and looking altogether as if he were cast	194
in iron.	196
The gentleman puffed, threw off his fur coat, sat down on the	208
bench, and said, "Which of you is the master bootmaker?"	218

Needs Work   1   2   3   4   5   Excellent
Paid attention to punctuation

Needs Work   1   2   3   4   5   Excellent
Sounded good

Total Words Read _____

Total Errors − _____

Correct WPM _____

57
Fiction

from "Holiday"
by Katherine Anne Porter

First Reading

	Words Read	Miscues

The wagon drew up before the porch, and I started climbing   11   _____

down. No sooner had my foot touched ground than an enormous   22   _____

black dog of the detestable German shepherd breed leaped silently   32   _____

at me, and as silently I covered my face with my arms and leaped   46   _____

back. "Kuno, down!" shouted the boy, lunging at him. The front   57   _____

door flew open and a young girl with yellow hair ran down the   70   _____

steps and seized the ugly beast by the scruff. "He does not mean   83   _____

anything," she said seriously in English. "He is only a dog."   94   _____

Just Louise's darling little puppy Kuno, I thought, a year or so   106   _____

older. Kuno whined, apologized by bowing and scraping one front   116   _____

paw on the ground, and the girl holding his scruff said, shyly and   129   _____

proudly, "I teach him that. He has always such bad manners, but   141   _____

I teach him!"   144   _____

I had arrived, it seemed, at the moment when the evening chores   156   _____

were about to begin. The entire Müller household streamed out   166   _____

of the door, each man and woman going about the affairs of the   179   _____

moment. The young girl walked with me up the porch and said,   191   _____

"This is my brother Hans," and a young man paused to shake   203   _____

hands and passed by.   207   _____

Needs Work   1   2   3   4   5   Excellent
Paid attention to punctuation

Needs Work   1   2   3   4   5   Excellent
Sounded good

Total Words Read   _____

Total Errors   − _____

Correct WPM   _____

from **"Holiday"**

by Katherine Anne Porter

	Words Read	Miscues

The wagon drew up before the porch, and I started climbing 11 _____

down. No sooner had my foot touched ground than an enormous 22 _____

black dog of the detestable German shepherd breed leaped silently 32 _____

at me, and as silently I covered my face with my arms and leaped 46 _____

back. "Kuno, down!" shouted the boy, lunging at him. The front 57 _____

door flew open and a young girl with yellow hair ran down the 70 _____

steps and seized the ugly beast by the scruff. "He does not mean 83 _____

anything," she said seriously in English. "He is only a dog." 94 _____

Just Louise's darling little puppy Kuno, I thought, a year or so 106 _____

older. Kuno whined, apologized by bowing and scraping one front 116 _____

paw on the ground, and the girl holding his scruff said, shyly and 129 _____

proudly, "I teach him that. He has always such bad manners, but 141 _____

I teach him!" 144 _____

I had arrived, it seemed, at the moment when the evening chores 156 _____

were about to begin. The entire Müller household streamed out 166 _____

of the door, each man and woman going about the affairs of the 179 _____

moment. The young girl walked with me up the porch and said, 191 _____

"This is my brother Hans," and a young man paused to shake 203 _____

hands and passed by. 207 _____

Needs Work   1   2   3   4   5   Excellent
_____
        Paid attention to punctuation

Needs Work   1   2   3   4   5   Excellent
_____
             Sounded good

Total Words Read   _____

Total Errors   −   _____

Correct WPM   _____

58 from *The Story of My Life*
by Helen Keller

Nonfiction

	Words Read	Miscues

She brought me my hat, and I knew I was going out into the   14 _____

warm sunshine. This thought, if a wordless sensation may be   24 _____

called a thought, made me hop and skip with pleasure.   34 _____

We walked down the path to the well-house, attracted by the   45 _____

fragrance of the honeysuckle with which it was covered. Some   55 _____

one was drawing water and my teacher placed my hand under the   67 _____

spout. As the cool stream gushed over one hand she spelled into   79 _____

the other the word *water,* first slowly, then rapidly. I stood still, my   92 _____

whole attention fixed upon the motions of her fingers. Suddenly I   103 _____

felt a misty consciousness as of something forgotten—a thrill of   114 _____

returning thought; and somehow the mystery of language was   123 _____

revealed to me. I knew then that "w-a-t-e-r" meant the wonderful   134 _____

cool something that was flowing over my hand. That living word   145 _____

awakened my soul, gave it light, hope, joy, set it free! There were   158 _____

barriers still, it is true, but barriers that could in time be swept   171 _____

away.   172 _____

I left the well-house eager to learn. Everything had a name, and   184 _____

each name gave birth to a new thought. As we returned to the   197 _____

house every object which I touched seemed to quiver with life.   208 _____

Needs Work   1   2   3   4   5   Excellent
Paid attention to punctuation

Needs Work   1   2   3   4   5   Excellent
Sounded good

Total Words Read   _____

Total Errors   –   _____

Correct WPM   _____

from *The Story of My Life*
by Helen Keller

	Words Read	Miscues

She brought me my hat, and I knew I was going out into the | 14 | _____

warm sunshine. This thought, if a wordless sensation may be | 24 | _____

called a thought, made me hop and skip with pleasure. | 34 | _____

We walked down the path to the well-house, attracted by the | 45 | _____

fragrance of the honeysuckle with which it was covered. Some | 55 | _____

one was drawing water and my teacher placed my hand under the | 67 | _____

spout. As the cool stream gushed over one hand she spelled into | 79 | _____

the other the word *water*, first slowly, then rapidly. I stood still, my | 92 | _____

whole attention fixed upon the motions of her fingers. Suddenly I | 103 | _____

felt a misty consciousness as of something forgotten—a thrill of | 114 | _____

returning thought; and somehow the mystery of language was | 123 | _____

revealed to me. I knew then that "w-a-t-e-r" meant the wonderful | 134 | _____

cool something that was flowing over my hand. That living word | 145 | _____

awakened my soul, gave it light, hope, joy, set it free! There were | 158 | _____

barriers still, it is true, but barriers that could in time be swept | 171 | _____

away. | 172 | _____

I left the well-house eager to learn. Everything had a name, and | 184 | _____

each name gave birth to a new thought. As we returned to the | 197 | _____

house every object which I touched seemed to quiver with life. | 208 | _____

Needs Work 1 2 3 4 5 Excellent
Paid attention to punctuation

Needs Work 1 2 3 4 5 Excellent
Sounded good

Total Words Read _____

Total Errors − _____

Correct WPM _____

59
Nonfiction

from *Give Me Liberty!*
The Story of the Declaration of Independence
by Russell Freedman

	Words Read	Miscues

William Gray, a master rope maker, knew there was going to be | 12 | _____

trouble in Boston that night. He wanted no part of it. As dusk fell, | 26 | _____

he closed the shutters of his house and shop. After supper, he sent | 39 | _____

his apprentice, fourteen-year-old Peter Slater, upstairs and locked | 47 | _____

the boy in his room. | 52 | _____

Peter waited until the house was quiet. Then he knotted his | 63 | _____

bedding together, hung it out the window, and slid to freedom. | 74 | _____

He wasn't a rope maker's apprentice for nothing. | 82 | _____

He hurried along dark cobbled streets to a secret meeting place, | 93 | _____

a blacksmith's shop where a crowd of men and boys seemed to be | 106 | _____

getting ready for a costume party. They were smearing their faces | 117 | _____

with coal dust and red paint and wrapping old blankets around | 128 | _____

their shoulders, disguising themselves as Mohawk Indians. | 135 | _____

Carrying hatchets and clubs, the "Indians" emerged from hiding | 144 | _____

and marched to Griffin's Wharf, where three British merchant | 153 | _____

ships were tied up at the dock. The ships' holds were filled to | 166 | _____

bursting with 342 chests of fine blended tea, shipped from | 176 | _____

England by the East India Company and worth a king's ransom. | 187 | _____

Dozens of other men and boys were arriving at Griffin's Wharf | 198 | _____

from all over Boston. | 202 | _____

Needs Work   1   2   3   4   5   Excellent
Paid attention to punctuation

Needs Work   1   2   3   4   5   Excellent
Sounded good

Total Words Read _____

Total Errors − _____

Correct WPM _____

59

Nonfiction

from *Give Me Liberty!*
The Story of the Declaration of Independence
by Russell Freedman

	Words Read	Miscues

	Words Read	Miscues
William Gray, a master rope maker, knew there was going to be	12	_____
trouble in Boston that night. He wanted no part of it. As dusk fell,	26	_____
he closed the shutters of his house and shop. After supper, he sent	39	_____
his apprentice, fourteen-year-old Peter Slater, upstairs and locked	47	_____
the boy in his room.	52	_____
Peter waited until the house was quiet. Then he knotted his	63	_____
bedding together, hung it out the window, and slid to freedom.	74	_____
He wasn't a rope maker's apprentice for nothing.	82	_____
He hurried along dark cobbled streets to a secret meeting place,	93	_____
a blacksmith's shop where a crowd of men and boys seemed to be	106	_____
getting ready for a costume party. They were smearing their faces	117	_____
with coal dust and red paint and wrapping old blankets around	128	_____
their shoulders, disguising themselves as Mohawk Indians.	135	_____
Carrying hatchets and clubs, the "Indians" emerged from hiding	144	_____
and marched to Griffin's Wharf, where three British merchant	153	_____
ships were tied up at the dock. The ships' holds were filled to	166	_____
bursting with 342 chests of fine blended tea, shipped from	176	_____
England by the East India Company and worth a king's ransom.	187	_____
Dozens of other men and boys were arriving at Griffin's Wharf	198	_____
from all over Boston.	202	_____

Needs Work   1   2   3   4   5   Excellent
Paid attention to punctuation

Needs Work   1   2   3   4   5   Excellent
Sounded good

Total Words Read   _____

Total Errors — _____

Correct WPM   _____

60

Nonfiction

Georgia O'Keeffe: Desert Artist

First Reading

	Words Read	Miscues

Georgia O'Keeffe is best known today for her abstract paintings — 10 — _____
of Southwestern landscapes and for her large, colorful flower — 19 — _____
paintings. Early in her career in New York, she won a prize for a — 33 — _____
detailed painting of a dead rabbit lying next to a shiny copper pot. — 46 — _____
In spite of this, O'Keeffe was not satisfied with her work. She felt — 59 — _____
that realism limited her creativity. — 64 — _____

Several years later, O'Keeffe took a summer art class. There, — 74 — _____
she was introduced to a new idea—that artwork should express — 85 — _____
the artist's ideas and feelings, not just mirror reality. This approach — 96 — _____
made sense to her. — 100 — _____

O'Keeffe moved to West Texas, where she fell in love with the — 112 — _____
desert. She became excited by art's possibilities. — 119 — _____

After awhile, O'Keeffe sent some of her drawings to New York. — 130 — _____
The drawings were abstract and unusual. Alfred Stieglitz, the — 139 — _____
famous photographer, insisted on exhibiting her artwork. His — 147 — _____
interest and excitement set her career in motion. — 155 — _____

The two artists quickly fell in love and married in 1924. They — 167 — _____
settled in New York, but Georgia spent the summers by herself in — 179 — _____
New Mexico. There she created many of her best-loved paintings. — 189 — _____

After Alfred died in 1946, O'Keeffe moved to New Mexico — 199 — _____
permanently. When she died at the age of 98, her ashes were — 211 — _____
scattered from the top of her favorite mountain, over the land — 222 — _____
she loved. — 224 — _____

Needs Work   1 2 3 4 5   Excellent
Paid attention to punctuation

Needs Work   1 2 3 4 5   Excellent
Sounded good

Total Words Read _____

Total Errors − _____

Correct WPM _____

Georgia O'Keeffe: Desert Artist

	Words Read	Miscues

Georgia O'Keeffe is best known today for her abstract paintings | 10 | _____
of Southwestern landscapes and for her large, colorful flower | 19 | _____
paintings. Early in her career in New York, she won a prize for a | 33 | _____
detailed painting of a dead rabbit lying next to a shiny copper pot. | 46 | _____
In spite of this, O'Keeffe was not satisfied with her work. She felt | 59 | _____
that realism limited her creativity. | 64 | _____

Several years later, O'Keeffe took a summer art class. There, | 74 | _____
she was introduced to a new idea—that artwork should express | 85 | _____
the artist's ideas and feelings, not just mirror reality. This approach | 96 | _____
made sense to her. | 100 | _____

O'Keeffe moved to West Texas, where she fell in love with the | 112 | _____
desert. She became excited by art's possibilities. | 119 | _____

After awhile, O'Keeffe sent some of her drawings to New York. | 130 | _____
The drawings were abstract and unusual. Alfred Stieglitz, the | 139 | _____
famous photographer, insisted on exhibiting her artwork. His | 147 | _____
interest and excitement set her career in motion. | 155 | _____

The two artists quickly fell in love and married in 1924. They | 167 | _____
settled in New York, but Georgia spent the summers by herself in | 179 | _____
New Mexico. There she created many of her best-loved paintings. | 189 | _____

After Alfred died in 1946, O'Keeffe moved to New Mexico | 199 | _____
permanently. When she died at the age of 98, her ashes were | 211 | _____
scattered from the top of her favorite mountain, over the land | 222 | _____
she loved. | 224 | _____

Needs Work   1   2   3   4   5   Excellent
Paid attention to punctuation

Needs Work   1   2   3   4   5   Excellent
Sounded good

Total Words Read _____

Total Errors − _____

Correct WPM _____

61
Fiction

from **"Waltz of the Fat Man"**
by Alberto Alvaro Rios

	Words Read	Miscues

One evening in winter as Noé was closing up his shop, having   12   _____

wound the clocks for the night and having left just enough heat in   25   _____

the stove that they would not suffer, he heard the blue clock falter.   38   _____

So much like a heartbeat had the sounds of the clocks come to be   52   _____

for him, that he was alarmed and stumbled in his quickness to   64   _____

reach the clock, though it could not move and was not falling.   76   _____

It called to him nonetheless as a wife in pain might call to her   90   _____

husband: honey, it said, please.   95   _____

He reached it too late, he thought, though it was simply a clock,   108   _____

and he laughed at himself.   113   _____

He tried winding the clock again, thinking the unthinkable, that   123   _____

perhaps he had missed its turn in his haste to leave. But that was   137   _____

not it: the spring was taut, and there was no play.   148   _____

He took it down from its nail, and looked at it from different   161   _____

angles in his hands, but he could see nothing extraordinary. There   172   _____

was no obvious damage, no one had dropped it without telling   183   _____

him and rehung it, no insect had been boring into its side. Its   196   _____

blue was still blue, without blemish.   202   _____

Needs Work   1   2   3   4   5   Excellent
Paid attention to punctuation

Needs Work   1   2   3   4   5   Excellent
Sounded good

Total Words Read   _____

Total Errors   – _____

Correct WPM   _____

from **"Waltz of the Fat Man"**
by Alberto Alvaro Rios

	Words Read	Miscues

One evening in winter as Noé was closing up his shop, having   12   _____
wound the clocks for the night and having left just enough heat in   25   _____
the stove that they would not suffer, he heard the blue clock falter.   38   _____
So much like a heartbeat had the sounds of the clocks come to be   52   _____
for him, that he was alarmed and stumbled in his quickness to   64   _____
reach the clock, though it could not move and was not falling.   76   _____
It called to him nonetheless as a wife in pain might call to her   90   _____
husband: honey, it said, please.   95   _____

He reached it too late, he thought, though it was simply a clock,   108   _____
and he laughed at himself.   113   _____

He tried winding the clock again, thinking the unthinkable, that   123   _____
perhaps he had missed its turn in his haste to leave. But that was   137   _____
not it: the spring was taut, and there was no play.   148   _____

He took it down from its nail, and looked at it from different   161   _____
angles in his hands, but he could see nothing extraordinary. There   172   _____
was no obvious damage, no one had dropped it without telling   183   _____
him and rehung it, no insect had been boring into its side. Its   196   _____
blue was still blue, without blemish.   202   _____

Needs Work   1   2   3   4   5   Excellent
Paid attention to punctuation

Needs Work   1   2   3   4   5   Excellent
Sounded good

Total Words Read   _____

Total Errors − _____

Correct WPM   _____

62
Nonfiction

from *Bully for You, Teddy Roosevelt!*
by Jean Fritz

	Words Read	Miscues

What did Theodore Roosevelt want to do? Everything. And all | 10 | _____
at once if possible. Plunging headlong into life, he refused to | 21 | _____
waste a single minute. Among other things, he studied birds, shot | 32 | _____
lions, roped steer, fought a war, wrote books, and discovered the | 43 | _____
source of a mystery river in South America. In addition, he | 54 | _____
became governor of New York, vice-president of the United | 63 | _____
States, then president. This was a big order for one man, but | 75 | _____
Theodore Roosevelt was not an everyday kind of man. He was so | 87 | _____
extraordinary that when people tried to describe him, they gave | 97 | _____
up on normal man-size words. "A cyclone," that's what Buffalo Bill | 108 | _____
called him. Mark Twain said he was "an earthquake." He was | 119 | _____
called "an eruption," "an express locomotive," "a buzz saw," | 128 | _____
"a dynamo." | 130 | _____

But he did not start out this way. Indeed, he was so puny that | 144 | _____
his parents worried if he would ever grow up at all. Born in New | 158 | _____
York City on October 27, 1858, Theodore (or Teddy, as he was | 170 | _____
called) was the second of the four Roosevelt children, and he was | 182 | _____
the sickly one, the one with asthma. As a child, he spent much of | 196 | _____
his time struggling just to get his breath. Often he would have to | 209 | _____
be propped up with pillows and would sit up in bed all night. | 222 | _____

Needs Work   1 2 3 4 5   Excellent
Paid attention to punctuation

Needs Work   1 2 3 4 5   Excellent
Sounded good

Total Words Read   _____

Total Errors   − _____

Correct WPM   _____

from *Bully for You, Teddy Roosevelt!*
by Jean Fritz

What did Theodore Roosevelt want to do? Everything. And all | 10 | _____

at once if possible. Plunging headlong into life, he refused to | 21 | _____

waste a single minute. Among other things, he studied birds, shot | 32 | _____

lions, roped steer, fought a war, wrote books, and discovered the | 43 | _____

source of a mystery river in South America. In addition, he | 54 | _____

became governor of New York, vice-president of the United | 63 | _____

States, then president. This was a big order for one man, but | 75 | _____

Theodore Roosevelt was not an everyday kind of man. He was so | 87 | _____

extraordinary that when people tried to describe him, they gave | 97 | _____

up on normal man-size words. "A cyclone," that's what Buffalo Bill | 108 | _____

called him. Mark Twain said he was "an earthquake." He was | 119 | _____

called "an eruption," "an express locomotive," "a buzz saw," | 128 | _____

"a dynamo." | 130 | _____

But he did not start out this way. Indeed, he was so puny that | 144 | _____

his parents worried if he would ever grow up at all. Born in New | 158 | _____

York City on October 27, 1858, Theodore (or Teddy, as he was | 170 | _____

called) was the second of the four Roosevelt children, and he was | 182 | _____

the sickly one, the one with asthma. As a child, he spent much of | 196 | _____

his time struggling just to get his breath. Often he would have to | 209 | _____

be propped up with pillows and would sit up in bed all night. | 222 | _____

Needs Work   1 2 3 4 5   Excellent
Paid attention to punctuation

Needs Work   1 2 3 4 5   Excellent
Sounded good

Total Words Read _____

Total Errors – _____

Correct WPM _____

63
Fiction

from **"The Jilting of Granny Weatherall"**
by Katherine Anne Porter

First Reading

	Words Read	Miscues

The thing that most annoyed [Granny] was that Cornelia thought   10   _____

she was deaf, dumb, and blind. Little hasty glances and tiny   21   _____

gestures tossed around her and over her head, saying, "Don't   31   _____

cross her, let her have her way, she's eighty years old," and she   44   _____

sitting there as if she lived in a thin glass cage. Sometimes Granny   57   _____

almost made up her mind to pack up and move back to her own   71   _____

house where nobody could remind her every minute that she was   82   _____

old. Wait, wait, Cornelia, till your own children whisper behind   92   _____

your back!   94   _____

    In her day she had kept a better house and had got more work   108   _____

done. She wasn't too old yet for Lydia to be driving eighty miles   121   _____

for advice when one of the children jumped the track, and Jimmy   133   _____

still dropped in and talked things over: "Now, Mammy, you've a   144   _____

good business head, I want to know what you think of this . . . ?"   156   _____

Old. Cornelia couldn't change the furniture round without asking.   165   _____

Little things, little things! They had been so sweet when they were   177   _____

little. Granny wished the old days were back again with the   188   _____

children young and everything to be done over.   196   _____

Needs Work   1 2 3 4 5   Excellent
Paid attention to punctuation

Needs Work   1 2 3 4 5   Excellent
Sounded good

Total Words Read _____

Total Errors − _____

Correct WPM _____

63
Fiction

from "The Jilting of Granny Weatherall"

by Katherine Anne Porter

	Words Read	Miscues

The thing that most annoyed [Granny] was that Cornelia thought — 10 — _____

she was deaf, dumb, and blind. Little hasty glances and tiny — 21 — _____

gestures tossed around her and over her head, saying, "Don't — 31 — _____

cross her, let her have her way, she's eighty years old," and she — 44 — _____

sitting there as if she lived in a thin glass cage. Sometimes Granny — 57 — _____

almost made up her mind to pack up and move back to her own — 71 — _____

house where nobody could remind her every minute that she was — 82 — _____

old. Wait, wait, Cornelia, till your own children whisper behind — 92 — _____

your back! — 94 — _____

In her day she had kept a better house and had got more work — 108 — _____

done. She wasn't too old yet for Lydia to be driving eighty miles — 121 — _____

for advice when one of the children jumped the track, and Jimmy — 133 — _____

still dropped in and talked things over: "Now, Mammy, you've a — 144 — _____

good business head, I want to know what you think of this . . . ?" — 156 — _____

Old. Cornelia couldn't change the furniture round without asking. — 165 — _____

Little things, little things! They had been so sweet when they were — 177 — _____

little. Granny wished the old days were back again with the — 188 — _____

children young and everything to be done over. — 196 — _____

Needs Work   1   2   3   4   5   Excellent
Paid attention to punctuation

Needs Work   1   2   3   4   5   Excellent
Sounded good

Total Words Read   _____

Total Errors   − _____

Correct WPM   _____

64

Fiction

from *Shane*
by Jack Schaefer

First Reading

	Words Read	Miscues

I crept along the corral fence, keeping tight to it, until I reached — 13 ——

the road. As soon as I was around the corner of the corral — 26 ——

with it and the barn between me and the pasture, I started — 38 ——

to run as rapidly as I could toward town, my feet plumping softly — 51 ——

in the thick dust of the road. I walked this every school day and it — 66 ——

had never seemed long before. Now the distance stretched ahead, — 76 ——

lengthening in my mind as if to mock me. — 85 ——

    I could not let [Shane] see me. I kept looking back over my — 98 ——

shoulder as I ran. When I saw him swinging into the road, I was — 112 ——

well past Johnson's, almost past Shipstead's, striking into the last — 122 ——

open stretch to the edge of town. I scurried to the side of the — 136 ——

road and behind a clump of bullberry bushes. Panting to get my — 148 ——

breath, I crouched there and waited for him to pass. The — 159 ——

hoofbeats swelled in my ears, mingled with the pounding beat of — 170 ——

my own blood. In my imagination he was galloping furiously and — 181 ——

I was positive he was already rushing past me. But when I parted — 194 ——

the bushes and pushed forward to peer out, he was moving at a — 207 ——

moderate pace. — 209 ——

Needs Work 1 2 3 4 5 Excellent
Paid attention to punctuation

Needs Work 1 2 3 4 5 Excellent
Sounded good

Total Words Read _____

Total Errors − _____

Correct WPM _____

from *Shane*

by Jack Schaefer

	Words Read	Miscues
I crept along the corral fence, keeping tight to it, until I reached	13	_____
the road. As soon as I was around the corner of the corral	26	_____
with it and the barn between me and the pasture, I started	38	_____
to run as rapidly as I could toward town, my feet plumping softly	51	_____
in the thick dust of the road. I walked this every school day and it	66	_____
had never seemed long before. Now the distance stretched ahead,	76	_____
lengthening in my mind as if to mock me.	85	_____
I could not let [Shane] see me. I kept looking back over my	98	_____
shoulder as I ran. When I saw him swinging into the road, I was	112	_____
well past Johnson's, almost past Shipstead's, striking into the last	122	_____
open stretch to the edge of town. I scurried to the side of the	136	_____
road and behind a clump of bullberry bushes. Panting to get my	148	_____
breath, I crouched there and waited for him to pass. The	159	_____
hoofbeats swelled in my ears, mingled with the pounding beat of	170	_____
my own blood. In my imagination he was galloping furiously and	181	_____
I was positive he was already rushing past me. But when I parted	194	_____
the bushes and pushed forward to peer out, he was moving at a	207	_____
moderate pace.	209	_____

Needs Work   1   2   3   4   5   Excellent
Paid attention to punctuation

Needs Work   1   2   3   4   5   Excellent
Sounded good

Total Words Read _____

Total Errors − _____

Correct WPM _____

from "A River Runs Through It"

65

Fiction

by Norman Maclean

	Words Read	Miscues

My father and mother were in retirement now, and neither | 10 | ———

one liked "being out of things," especially my mother, who was | 21 | ———

younger than my father and was used to "running the church." To | 33 | ———

them, Paul was the reporter, their chief contact with reality, the | 44 | ———

recorder of the world that was leaving them and that they had | 56 | ———

never known very well anyway. He had to tell them story after | 68 | ———

story, even though they did not approve of some of them. We sat | 81 | ———

around the table a long time. As we started to get up, I said to | 96 | ———

Father, "We'd appreciate it if you would go fishing with us | 107 | ———

tomorrow." | 108 | ———

"Oh," my father said and sat down again, automatically | 117 | ———

unfolded his napkin, and asked, "Are you sure, Paul, that you | 128 | ———

want me? I can't fish some of those big holes anymore. I can't | 141 | ———

wade anymore." | 143 | ———

Paul said, "Sure I want you. Whenever you can get near fish, | 155 | ———

you can catch them." | 159 | ———

To my father, the highest commandment was to do whatever his | 170 | ———

sons wanted him to do, especially if it meant to go fishing. The | 183 | ———

minister looked as if his congregation had just asked him to come | 195 | ———

back and preach his farewell sermon over again. | 203 | ———

Needs Work   1 2 3 4 5   Excellent
_____
Paid attention to punctuation

Needs Work   1 2 3 4 5   Excellent
_____
Sounded good

Total Words Read _____

Total Errors − _____

Correct WPM _____

from "A River Runs Through It"
by Norman Maclean

	Words Read	Miscues
My father and mother were in retirement now, and neither	10	___
one liked "being out of things," especially my mother, who was	21	___
younger than my father and was used to "running the church." To	33	___
them, Paul was the reporter, their chief contact with reality, the	44	___
recorder of the world that was leaving them and that they had	56	___
never known very well anyway. He had to tell them story after	68	___
story, even though they did not approve of some of them. We sat	81	___
around the table a long time. As we started to get up, I said to	96	___
Father, "We'd appreciate it if you would go fishing with us	107	___
tomorrow."	108	___
"Oh," my father said and sat down again, automatically	117	___
unfolded his napkin, and asked, "Are you sure, Paul, that you	128	___
want me? I can't fish some of those big holes anymore. I can't	141	___
wade anymore."	143	___
Paul said, "Sure I want you. Whenever you can get near fish,	155	___
you can catch them."	159	___
To my father, the highest commandment was to do whatever his	170	___
sons wanted him to do, especially if it meant to go fishing. The	183	___
minister looked as if his congregation had just asked him to come	195	___
back and preach his farewell sermon over again.	203	___

Needs Work   1   2   3   4   5   Excellent
Paid attention to punctuation

Needs Work   1   2   3   4   5   Excellent
Sounded good

Total Words Read _____

Total Errors − _____

Correct WPM _____

66

Nonfiction

from *Bill Peet: An Autobiography*
by Bill Peet

	Words Read	Miscues

Grandmother suddenly called out from her bedroom, a loud, — 9

mournful wail that echoed all through the house. — 17

In a panic we rushed upstairs to the foot of her bed just as — 31

she made one last desperate gasp for breath, then died of a — 43

heart attack. — 45

My mother, my brothers, and I were devastated. It was hard to — 57

believe that my grandmother was gone, and so suddenly. — 66

That horrifying moment of watching her die haunted me for — 76

many years. — 78

Soon after Grandmother's death her house was sold so the — 88

money could be divided among the heirs. — 95

Moving out of 518 North Riley Avenue was a painful uprooting, — 106

and after that we would be renting and moving many times, and — 118

we would always be strangers in the neighborhood. — 126

It was a miserable time to be starting Tech High School, which — 138

was one of the biggest high schools in the country. — 148

Entering the campus was like being lost in a foreign city — 159

without a familiar face in sight. — 165

But then many of my grade school classmates couldn't afford — 175

to go on to high school in those hard times—they had to go out — 190

and find a job. I shouldn't have been going to high school either. — 203

Needs Work   1 2 3 4 5   Excellent
Paid attention to punctuation

Needs Work   1 2 3 4 5   Excellent
Sounded good

Total Words Read _____

Total Errors − _____

Correct WPM _____

from *Bill Peet: An Autobiography*

by Bill Peet

	Words Read	Miscues
Grandmother suddenly called out from her bedroom, a loud,	9	_____
mournful wail that echoed all through the house.	17	_____
In a panic we rushed upstairs to the foot of her bed just as	31	_____
she made one last desperate gasp for breath, then died of a	43	_____
heart attack.	45	_____
My mother, my brothers, and I were devastated. It was hard to	57	_____
believe that my grandmother was gone, and so suddenly.	66	_____
That horrifying moment of watching her die haunted me for	76	_____
many years.	78	_____
Soon after Grandmother's death her house was sold so the	88	_____
money could be divided among the heirs.	95	_____
Moving out of 518 North Riley Avenue was a painful uprooting,	106	_____
and after that we would be renting and moving many times, and	118	_____
we would always be strangers in the neighborhood.	126	_____
It was a miserable time to be starting Tech High School, which	138	_____
was one of the biggest high schools in the country.	148	_____
Entering the campus was like being lost in a foreign city	159	_____
without a familiar face in sight.	165	_____
But then many of my grade school classmates couldn't afford	175	_____
to go on to high school in those hard times—they had to go out	190	_____
and find a job. I shouldn't have been going to high school either.	203	_____

Needs Work   1   2   3   4   5   Excellent
Paid attention to punctuation

Needs Work   1   2   3   4   5   Excellent
Sounded good

Total Words Read _____

Total Errors − _____

Correct WPM _____

Renoir

67

Nonfiction

	Words Read	Miscues

On February 25, 1841, Pierre Auguste Renoir was born in France, in a town famous for its fine porcelain. Young Renoir showed an early talent for art, so his family sent him to learn how to paint designs on dishes and vases.

In 1854, at the age of thirteen, Renoir went to Paris, where he painted designs on window shades and fans. He also took art lessons, and in the studio he met other young artists. One was Claude Monet, who became a good friend, and later, one of the world's great artists.

Renoir and Monet experimented with creating the effect of a color by dabbing different colors next to each other. The style they developed was called impressionism. But Renoir wanted to do other things. He went to Italy, where he developed his interests in drawing and painting people. His most famous works are those of the people whose portraits he painted.

In his old age, Renoir developed painful arthritis. But he did not let swollen joints stop him. He had his assistants tie the brush to his hands so he could continue to paint. His final paintings are done in wide, bold brush strokes and brilliant colors.

Words Read
10
21
35
42
55
66
78
90
93
103
114
123
135
146
153
164
177
190
199

Needs Work   1   2   3   4   5   Excellent
Paid attention to punctuation

Needs Work   1   2   3   4   5   Excellent
Sounded good

Total Words Read _____

Total Errors − _____

Correct WPM _____

Renoir

	Words Read	Miscues

On February 25, 1841, Pierre Auguste Renoir was born in — 10
France, in a town famous for its fine porcelain. Young Renoir — 21
showed an early talent for art, so his family sent him to learn how — 35
to paint designs on dishes and vases. — 42

In 1854, at the age of thirteen, Renoir went to Paris, where he — 55
painted designs on window shades and fans. He also took art — 66
lessons, and in the studio he met other young artists. One was — 78
Claude Monet, who became a good friend, and later, one of the — 90
world's great artists. — 93

Renoir and Monet experimented with creating the effect of a — 103
color by dabbing different colors next to each other. The style — 114
they developed was called impressionism. But Renoir wanted to — 123
do other things. He went to Italy, where he developed his interests — 135
in drawing and painting people. His most famous works are those — 146
of the people whose portraits he painted. — 153

In his old age, Renoir developed painful arthritis. But he did — 164
not let swollen joints stop him. He had his assistants tie the brush — 177
to his hands so he could continue to paint. His final paintings are — 190
done in wide, bold brush strokes and brilliant colors. — 199

Needs Work   1 2 3 4 5   Excellent
Paid attention to punctuation

Needs Work   1 2 3 4 5   Excellent
Sounded good

Total Words Read _____

Total Errors − _____

Correct WPM _____

68
Fiction

from *Animal Farm*
by George Orwell

	Words Read	Miscues

The singing of [the] song threw the animals into the wildest — 11

excitement. Almost before Major had reached the end, they had — 21

begun singing it for themselves. Even the stupidest of them had — 32

already picked up the tune and a few of the words, and as for the — 47

clever ones, such as the pigs and dogs, they had the entire song by — 61

heart within a few minutes. And then, after a few preliminary tries, — 73

the whole farm burst out into "Beasts of England" in tremendous — 84

unison. The cows lowed it, the dogs whined it, the sheep bleated — 96

it, the horses whinnied it, the ducks quacked it. They were so — 108

delighted with the song that they sang it right through five times — 120

in succession, and might have continued singing it all night if they — 132

had not been interrupted. — 136

Unfortunately the uproar awoke Mr. Jones, who sprang out of — 146

bed, making sure that there was a fox in the yard. He seized the — 160

gun which always stood in a corner of his bedroom, and let fly a — 174

charge of Number 6 shot into the darkness. The pellets buried — 185

themselves in the wall of the barn and the meeting broke up — 197

hurriedly. Everyone fled to his own sleeping-place. — 204

Needs Work 1 2 3 4 5 Excellent
Paid attention to punctuation

Needs Work 1 2 3 4 5 Excellent
Sounded good

Total Words Read _____

Total Errors − _____

Correct WPM _____

from ***Animal Farm***
by George Orwell

	Words Read	Miscues

The singing of [the] song threw the animals into the wildest   11   _____

excitement. Almost before Major had reached the end, they had   21   _____

begun singing it for themselves. Even the stupidest of them had   32   _____

already picked up the tune and a few of the words, and as for the   47   _____

clever ones, such as the pigs and dogs, they had the entire song by   61   _____

heart within a few minutes. And then, after a few preliminary tries,   73   _____

the whole farm burst out into "Beasts of England" in tremendous   84   _____

unison. The cows lowed it, the dogs whined it, the sheep bleated   96   _____

it, the horses whinnied it, the ducks quacked it. They were so   108   _____

delighted with the song that they sang it right through five times   120   _____

in succession, and might have continued singing it all night if they   132   _____

had not been interrupted.   136   _____

Unfortunately the uproar awoke Mr. Jones, who sprang out of   146   _____

bed, making sure that there was a fox in the yard. He seized the   160   _____

gun which always stood in a corner of his bedroom, and let fly a   174   _____

charge of Number 6 shot into the darkness. The pellets buried   185   _____

themselves in the wall of the barn and the meeting broke up   197   _____

hurriedly. Everyone fled to his own sleeping-place.   204   _____

Needs Work   1   2   3   4   5   Excellent
Paid attention to punctuation

Needs Work   1   2   3   4   5   Excellent
Sounded good

Total Words Read   _____

Total Errors   − _____

Correct WPM   _____

69 The Lincoln Highway

Nonfiction

	Words Read	Miscues

In 1912 two pioneers in the automobile business, Carl Fisher   10 _____
and Henry Joy, proposed building a cross-country road. Fisher   19 _____
and Joy planned to get the job done by 1915. People with cars   32 _____
would then find it easier to drive to the San Francisco Exposition.   44 _____
Fisher and Joy suggested calling the road the Lincoln Highway. To   55 _____
promote their idea, they formed the Lincoln Highway Association.   64 _____

The Lincoln Highway was a rough patchwork of existing roads.   74 _____
It wound through acres of cornfields and along the main streets   85 _____
of small towns. But people liked the idea. Businesses competed   95 _____
for an address on the Lincoln Highway.   102 _____

By 1924 Iowans were paving their section of the Lincoln   112 _____
Highway. Farmers were moving more produce on the road, and   122 _____
more people were traveling by car. The idea grew, and more   133 _____
highways were developed.   136 _____

In 1925 the United States government decided that named   145 _____
highways were too confusing. They began labeling them with   154 _____
numbers. The Lincoln Highway Association was disbanded in   162 _____
1928, but work on the highway went on and people kept using   174 _____
the Lincoln name. Today, Interstate 80 follows much the same   184 _____
route as the old Lincoln Highway, the forerunner of our national   195 _____
highway system.   197 _____

Needs Work   1   2   3   4   5   Excellent
_____
Paid attention to punctuation

Needs Work   1   2   3   4   5   Excellent
_____
Sounded good

Total Words Read   _____

Total Errors − _____

Correct WPM   _____

The Lincoln Highway

	Words Read	Miscues

In 1912 two pioneers in the automobile business, Carl Fisher | 10 | _____
and Henry Joy, proposed building a cross-country road. Fisher | 19 | _____
and Joy planned to get the job done by 1915. People with cars | 32 | _____
would then find it easier to drive to the San Francisco Exposition. | 44 | _____
Fisher and Joy suggested calling the road the Lincoln Highway. To | 55 | _____
promote their idea, they formed the Lincoln Highway Association. | 64 | _____

The Lincoln Highway was a rough patchwork of existing roads. | 74 | _____
It wound through acres of cornfields and along the main streets | 85 | _____
of small towns. But people liked the idea. Businesses competed | 95 | _____
for an address on the Lincoln Highway. | 102 | _____

By 1924 Iowans were paving their section of the Lincoln | 112 | _____
Highway. Farmers were moving more produce on the road, and | 122 | _____
more people were traveling by car. The idea grew, and more | 133 | _____
highways were developed. | 136 | _____

In 1925 the United States government decided that named | 145 | _____
highways were too confusing. They began labeling them with | 154 | _____
numbers. The Lincoln Highway Association was disbanded in | 162 | _____
1928, but work on the highway went on and people kept using | 174 | _____
the Lincoln name. Today, Interstate 80 follows much the same | 184 | _____
route as the old Lincoln Highway, the forerunner of our national | 195 | _____
highway system. | 197 | _____

Needs Work   1 2 3 4 5   Excellent
Paid attention to punctuation

Needs Work   1 2 3 4 5   Excellent
Sounded good

Total Words Read _____

Total Errors − _____

Correct WPM _____

70

Nonfiction

from *The Autobiography of Benjamin Franklin*

by Benjamin Franklin

First Reading

	Words Read	Miscues
I walked toward the top of the street, gazing about till near	12	_____
Market Street, when I met a boy with bread. I had often made a	26	_____
meal of dry bread, and inquiring where he had bought it, I went	39	_____
immediately to the baker's he directed me to. I asked for biscuits,	51	_____
meaning such as we had at Boston; that sort, it seems, was not	64	_____
made at Philadelphia. I then asked for a three-penny loaf and was	76	_____
told they had none. Not knowing the different prices nor the	87	_____
names for the different sorts of bread, I told him to give me	100	_____
three-penny worth of any sort. He gave me accordingly three great	111	_____
puffy rolls. I was surprised at the quantity, but took it, and having	124	_____
no room in my pockets, walked off with a roll under each arm	137	_____
and eating the other. Thus I went up Market Street as far as	150	_____
Fourth Street, passing by the door of Mr. Read, my future wife's	162	_____
father; when she, standing at the door, saw me, and thought I	174	_____
made, as I certainly did, a most awkward, ridiculous appearance.	184	_____
Then I turned and went down Chestnut Street and part of	195	_____
Walnut Street, eating my roll all the way.	203	_____

Needs Work 1 2 3 4 5 Excellent
Paid attention to punctuation

Needs Work 1 2 3 4 5 Excellent
Sounded good

Total Words Read _____

Total Errors − _____

Correct WPM _____

from *The Autobiography of Benjamin Franklin*

by Benjamin Franklin

Second Reading

	Words Read	Miscues

I walked toward the top of the street, gazing about till near   12 _____

Market Street, when I met a boy with bread. I had often made a   26 _____

meal of dry bread, and inquiring where he had bought it, I went   39 _____

immediately to the baker's he directed me to. I asked for biscuits,   51 _____

meaning such as we had at Boston; that sort, it seems, was not   64 _____

made at Philadelphia. I then asked for a three-penny loaf and was   76 _____

told they had none. Not knowing the different prices nor the   87 _____

names for the different sorts of bread, I told him to give me   100 _____

three-penny worth of any sort. He gave me accordingly three great   111 _____

puffy rolls. I was surprised at the quantity, but took it, and having   124 _____

no room in my pockets, walked off with a roll under each arm   137 _____

and eating the other. Thus I went up Market Street as far as   150 _____

Fourth Street, passing by the door of Mr. Read, my future wife's   162 _____

father; when she, standing at the door, saw me, and thought I   174 _____

made, as I certainly did, a most awkward, ridiculous appearance.   184 _____

Then I turned and went down Chestnut Street and part of   195 _____

Walnut Street, eating my roll all the way.   203 _____

Needs Work   1   2   3   4   5   Excellent
Paid attention to punctuation

Needs Work   1   2   3   4   5   Excellent
Sounded good

Total Words Read   _____

Total Errors   – _____

Correct WPM   _____

71

Nonfiction

from *Charles A. Lindbergh: A Human Hero*

by James Cross Giblin

First Reading

	Words Read	Miscues

The fog started to thin, and suddenly the *Spirit of St. Louis* broke through to sunlight and blue sky. An hour or so later, after flying in and out of clouds and sun, Charles saw what he thought was a coastline down below. How could that be? By his own estimate he was at least a thousand miles from land. He dropped down to investigate and was disappointed to discover that the coastline was just a "fog island"—a mirage.

12	———
25	———
38	———
50	———
62	———
72	———
80	———

Back in the United States, hundreds of newspapers on that Saturday morning ran a column by the noted humorist Will Rogers. But on this occasion he struck a serious note. "No jokes today," the column began. "A slim, tall, bashful, smiling American boy is somewhere over the middle of the Atlantic Ocean, where no lone human being has ever ventured before. . . ."

90	———
100	———
112	———
122	———
133	———
141	———

At midday on Saturday a fresh wave of fatigue swept over Charles. His eyes closed and stayed shut for four, five, ten seconds before he managed to force them open. He slapped his face once, and then slapped it harder, counting on the stinging sensation to wake his body. But he barely felt either blow.

152	———
164	———
176	———
187	———
196	———

For the first time he doubted his ability to endure, to stay awake, to complete the flight.

208	———
213	———

Needs Work   1   2   3   4   5   Excellent
Paid attention to punctuation

Needs Work   1   2   3   4   5   Excellent
Sounded good

Total Words Read   _____

Total Errors   − _____

Correct WPM   _____

from *Charles A. Lindbergh: A Human Hero*

by James Cross Giblin

	Words Read	Miscues

The fog started to thin, and suddenly the *Spirit of St. Louis* | 12 | _____
broke through to sunlight and blue sky. An hour or so later, after | 25 | _____
flying in and out of clouds and sun, Charles saw what he thought | 38 | _____
was a coastline down below. How could that be? By his own | 50 | _____
estimate he was at least a thousand miles from land. He dropped | 62 | _____
down to investigate and was disappointed to discover that the | 72 | _____
coastline was just a "fog island"—a mirage. | 80 | _____

Back in the United States, hundreds of newspapers on that | 90 | _____
Saturday morning ran a column by the noted humorist Will | 100 | _____
Rogers. But on this occasion he struck a serious note. "No jokes | 112 | _____
today," the column began. "A slim, tall, bashful, smiling American | 122 | _____
boy is somewhere over the middle of the Atlantic Ocean, where | 133 | _____
no lone human being has ever ventured before. . . ." | 141 | _____

At midday on Saturday a fresh wave of fatigue swept over | 152 | _____
Charles. His eyes closed and stayed shut for four, five, ten seconds | 164 | _____
before he managed to force them open. He slapped his face once, | 176 | _____
and then slapped it harder, counting on the stinging sensation to | 187 | _____
wake his body. But he barely felt either blow. | 196 | _____

For the first time he doubted his ability to endure, to stay | 208 | _____
awake, to complete the flight. | 213 | _____

Needs Work 1 2 3 4 5 Excellent
Paid attention to punctuation

Needs Work 1 2 3 4 5 Excellent
Sounded good

Total Words Read _____

Total Errors − _____

Correct WPM _____

The American Dream

72

Nonfiction

First Reading

	Words Read	Miscues

∼∼∼

Early on the morning of April 19, 1775, Paul Revere raced past	12	————
the village green in Lexington, Massachusetts. He stopped just	21	————
down the street at a house where John Hancock and John Adams	33	————
were hiding from the British. Within minutes the town bell rang	44	————
out the alarm. Captain John Parker and his 70-man militia formed	55	————
two battle lines on the green. Four and a half hours later the "shot	69	————
heard round the world" shattered the morning's stillness. "If they	79	————
mean to have a war," Parker said, "let it begin here." The British	92	————
did not want a war and did not wish to start one, but it happened.	107	————
Two months passed before the American Revolution began in	116	————
earnest, but the fighting in this village by a small group of armed	129	————
Americans marked the beginning of a new era.	137	————
Spread across the mountains and valleys of the eastern United	147	————
States are the battlefields and roads where the two great armies	158	————
marched, the places they fortified, and the rivers they crossed.	168	————
Each site played a role in the drama that shaped and molded a	181	————
loosely knit group of colonies into a nation. Each helped form the	193	————
dream that became the United States.	199	————

Needs Work   1   2   3   4   5   Excellent
Paid attention to punctuation

Needs Work   1   2   3   4   5   Excellent
Sounded good

Total Words Read _____

Total Errors − _____

Correct WPM _____

The American Dream

	Words Read	Miscues

Early on the morning of April 19, 1775, Paul Revere raced past the village green in Lexington, Massachusetts. He stopped just down the street at a house where John Hancock and John Adams were hiding from the British. Within minutes the town bell rang out the alarm. Captain John Parker and his 70-man militia formed two battle lines on the green. Four and a half hours later the "shot heard round the world" shattered the morning's stillness. "If they mean to have a war," Parker said, "let it begin here." The British did not want a war and did not wish to start one, but it happened. Two months passed before the American Revolution began in earnest, but the fighting in this village by a small group of armed Americans marked the beginning of a new era.

Spread across the mountains and valleys of the eastern United States are the battlefields and roads where the two great armies marched, the places they fortified, and the rivers they crossed. Each site played a role in the drama that shaped and molded a loosely knit group of colonies into a nation. Each helped form the dream that became the United States.

Words Read
12
21
33
44
55
69
79
92
107
116
129
137
147
158
168
181
193
199

Needs Work 1 2 3 4 5 Excellent
Paid attention to punctuation

Needs Work 1 2 3 4 5 Excellent
Sounded good

Total Words Read _____

Total Errors − _____

Correct WPM _____

Progress Graph

1. For the first reading of the selection, put a red dot on the line above the selection number to show your correct words-per-minute rate.

2. For the second reading, put a blue dot on the line above the selection number to show your correct words-per-minute rate.

3. Make a graph to show your progress. Connect the red dots from selection to selection with red lines. Connect the blue dots with blue lines.

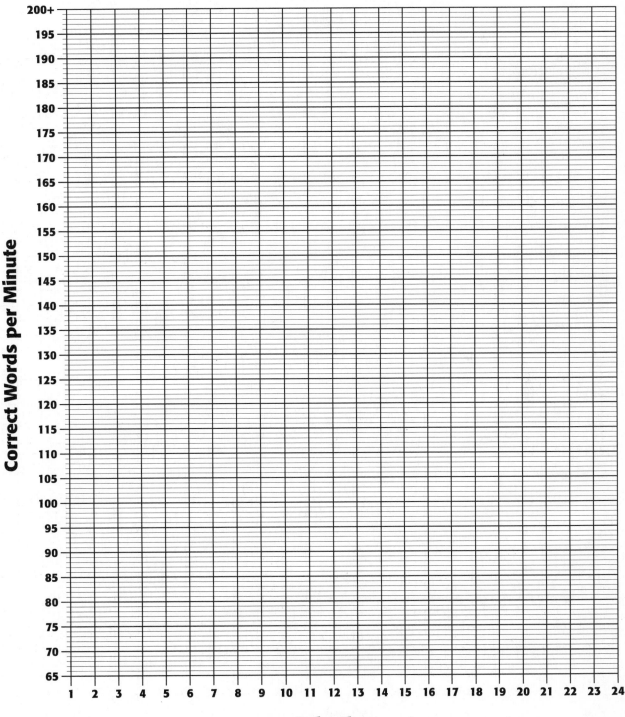

Correct Words per Minute

Selection

Progress Graph

1. For the first reading of the selection, put a red dot on the line above the selection number to show your correct words-per-minute rate.

2. For the second reading, put a blue dot on the line above the selection number to show your correct words-per-minute rate.

3. Make a graph to show your progress. Connect the red dots from selection to selection with red lines. Connect the blue dots with blue lines.

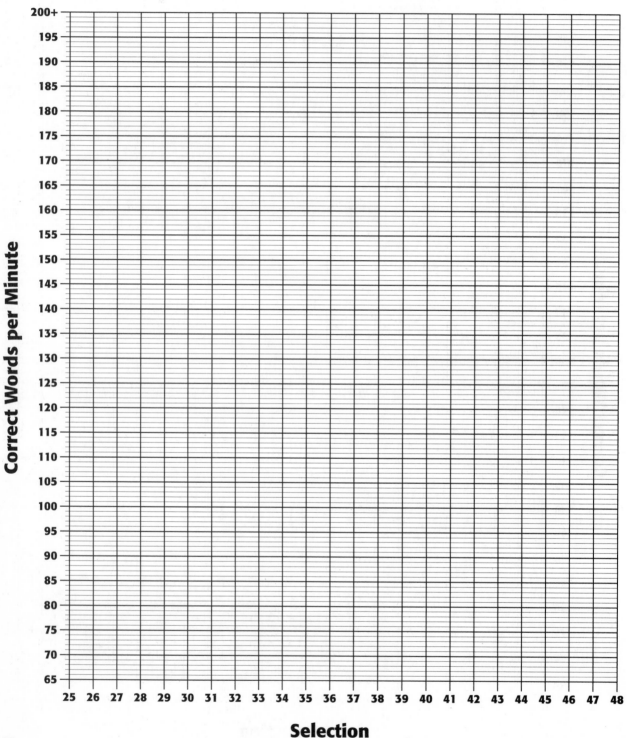

Correct Words per Minute

Selection

Progress Graph

1. For the first reading of the selection, put a red dot on the line above the selection number to show your correct words-per-minute rate.

2. For the second reading, put a blue dot on the line above the selection number to show your correct words-per-minute rate.

3. Make a graph to show your progress. Connect the red dots from selection to selection with red lines. Connect the blue dots with blue lines.

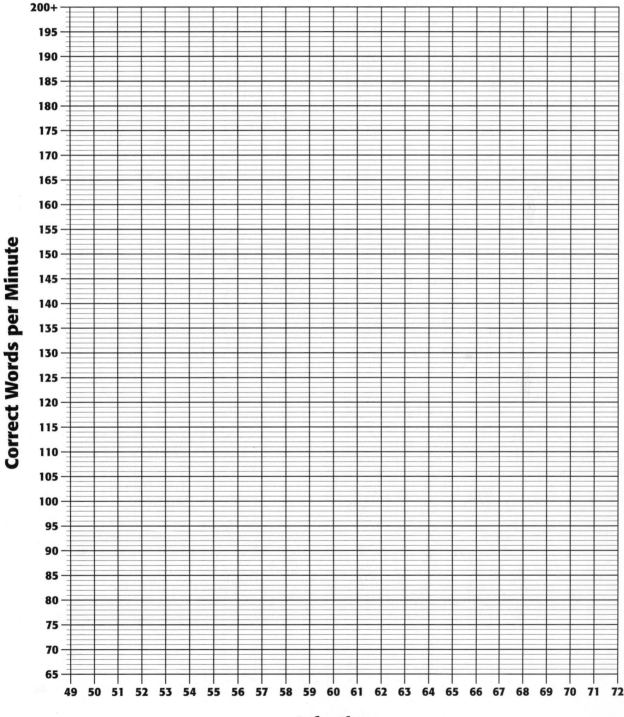

Selection

Acknowledgments

Grateful acknowledgment is given to the authors and publishers listed below for brief passages excerpted from these longer works.

from *Undying Glory* by Clinton Cox. Copyright © 1991 by Clinton Cox. Scholastic.

from "Waiting" from *The Leaving* by Budge Wilson. Copyright © 1990 by Budge Wilson. First American Edition, 1992, published by Philomel Books, a division of The Putnam & Grosset Group.

from *Anne Frank: The Diary of a Young Girl* by Anne Frank. Copyright © 1952 by Otto H. Frank. Doubleday, a division of Bantam Doubleday Dell Publishing Group, a division of Random House.

from *Hatchet* by Gary Paulsen. Copyright © 1987 by Gary Paulsen. Macmillan Books for Young Readers, an imprint of Simon & Schuster Children's Publishing Division, Simon & Schuster Macmillan.

from *The Lost Garden* by Laurence Yep. Copyright © 1991 by Laurence Yep. Julian Messner, a division of Silver Burdett Press, Inc. Simon & Schuster.

from "Three Days to See" by Helen Keller, from *The Atlantic Monthly*, vol. CLI, Jan.–June, 1933.

from *Farewell to Manzanar* by James D. and Jeanne Wakatsuki Houston. Copyright © 1973 by James D. Houston. Houghton Mifflin.

from *Sounder* by William H. Armstrong. Copyright © 1969 by William H. Armstrong. HarperCollins Publishers.

from "The Life You Save May Be Your Own" from *A Good Man Is Hard to Find and Other Stories* by Flannery O'Connor. Copyright © 1953 by Flannery O'Connor and renewed 1981 by Reginia O'Connor. Harcourt Brace.

from *On the Way Home* by Laura Ingalls Wilder and Rose Wilder Lane. Copyright © 1962 by Roger Lea MacBride. Harper & Row Junior Books.

from *Walt Whitman* by Catherine Reef. Copyright © 1995 by Catherine Reef. Clarion Books, an imprint of Houghton Mifflin.

from "Dragon, Dragon" from *Dragon, Dragon and Other Tales* by John Gardner. Copyright © 1975 by Boskydell Artists Ltd.

from *My Ántonia* by Willa Cather. Copyright © 1918, 1926, and 1946 by Willa Sibert Cather; copyright © 1954 by Edith Lewis. Houghton Mifflin.

from *A Brilliant Streak: The Making of Mark Twain* by Kathryn Lasky. Copyright © 1998 by Kathryn Lasky Knight. Harcourt Brace.

from *Portrait of Jennie* by Robert Nathan. Copyright © 1939, renewed 1967, by Robert Nathan. Alfred A. Knopf.

from *China Homecoming* by Jean Fritz. Copyright © 1985 by Jean Fritz. G. P. Putnam's Sons.

from *To Kill a Mockingbird* by Harper Lee. Copyright © 1960 and renewed 1988 by Harper Lee. HarperCollins Publishers.

from "The Medicine Bag" by Virginia Driving Hawk Sneve, from *Boys' Life*, March 1975.

from "Broken Chain" from *Baseball in April and Other Stories* by Gary Soto. Copyright © 1990 by Gary Soto. Harcourt Brace.

from "A Christmas Memory" from *Breakfast at Tiffany's* by Truman Capote. Copyright © 1956 and renewed 1984 by Truman Capote. Random House.

from "Two Kinds" by Amy Tan. Copyright © 1989 by Amy Tan.

from *When Plague Strikes: The Black Death, Smallpox, AIDS.* Copyright © 1995 by James Cross Giblin. HarperCollins Publishers.

from "A Crush" from *A Couple of Kooks and Other Stories About Love* by Cynthia Rylant. Copyright © 1990 by Cynthia Rylant. Orchard Books, New York.

from "Satchel Paige" from *Champions* by Bill Littlefield. Copyright © 1993 by Bill Littlefield. Little, Brown.

from "The Flat of the Land" by Diana Garcia. Copyright © 1992 by Diana Garcia.

from "A Christmas Carol" from *A Christmas Carol and Other Stories* by Charles Dickens. Modern Library Edition 1995, Random House.

from "I See the Promised Land" from *A Testament of Hope: The Essential Writings of Martin Luther King, Jr.* Copyright © 1968 by the Estate of Martin Luther King.